INDIA

AND

TIGER-HUNTING

INDIA
AND
TIGER-HUNTING

JULIUS BARRAS

GYAN

Published by

GYAN

Gyan Publishing House
5, Ansari Road
Daryaganj, New Delhi-110002
Phone: 011-47034999, 9811692060
E-mail: books@gyanbooks.com

Distribution Network
gyanbooks.com
India, USA, Canada, UK, Australia

ISBN: 978-93-7133-572-0 (HB)

First Published, 1883

2nd Impression 2025

Printed at: Gyan Press, Delhi.

INDIA AND TIGER-HUNTING
Author Julius Barras

INDIA

AND

TIGER-HUNTING.

INDIA

AND

TIGER-HUNTING.

BY

JULIUS BARRAS.

VOL. I.

TIGER-HUNTING AND OTHER ADVENTURES.

LONDON:
RASTALL & SON, 81 EBURY STREET.
1883.

DEDICATED

TO

MAJOR W. S. HORE,

WINNER OF

THE BHEEMA CUP.

PREFACE.

ALL who, like myself, have passed twenty-eight years of their lives in the army in India, must have met with many and strange adventures, but comparatively few will take the trouble to endeavour to relate them in print. They either do not care to face the labour, which is anything but light, or they fear to be disbelieved, which is necessarily very painful. Each of these considerations might have deterred me from coming before the public; but experience has shown me that there is really no escape from either dilemma. Amongst a numerous circle of friends I am constantly called upon to 'tell a tale.' I yield, and give myself much trouble to amuse the audience, and am apparently successful in this particular. I learn, however, in the course of time, that few, if any, of the listeners believed a syllable of what they had heard. This was considerably mortifying, when I had carefully avoided even the most trivial exaggeration for the sake of heightening the effect. In vain I wrapped myself in gloomy silence, resolved never to mention a single personal experience again. This frame of mind only made people more resolved than ever to draw me out ; so, without any idea that my doings were more remarkable than those of average persons similarly situated, I at last thought the best and least tiresome course would be to write a couple of volumes, which should contain a strictly veracious account of the principal adventures of my life in the East,—an account which should not only be true, but easily capable of verification by any reader who might care to take the slightest pains to such an end.

As nothing can be more dreary than life in an Indian military cantonment, it will surprise no one to learn that sporting incidents, such as tiger-shooting, and wolf-hunting with greyhounds, will form the chief attraction of the present work. That the facts recorded may prove sufficiently exciting to interest the general reader, and yet so correctly recorded as to afford much useful information to young and consequently inexperienced sportsmen, is my object in presenting this work to the public.

TIGER-HUNTING

AND

ADVENTURES IN INDIA.

CHAPTER I.

IT is not my intention to try the reader's patience by describing exactly how and when I landed in India, or my first impression concerning the country and its people. At first I had so much to do in preparing to pass sundry examinations insisted upon by my exacting employers, that I really had no time to look at views, or to think of any sport. True, I did, during my leisure moments, try to study the characters of the four servants who formed my modest establishment, but this soon ended in my discovering that they had none—never had had any. The dozen or two written ones with which each was provided at the time I had engaged him, had been hired for the day in the Bazaar, at a cost of four annas, which is rather less than sixpence.

As soon, however, as I could, I set off into the jungles, and in them I spent as much time as was possible during the whole of my residence in India. Tiger-shooting was my principal amusement, and, as it is an expensive pastime, I think I cannot begin better than by pointing out a few of the more costly preparations which must be made before this sport can be indulged in, and by also indicating a few contingencies that may easily arise, and cost the adventurer a good deal more than he may have anticipated.

For tiger-shooting the best and most highly finished weapons are indispensable. What, for instance, is the use of the finest lock and barrels if the wood of the stock is not sufficiently seasoned to bear, without warping, the fierce heat to which it is exposed under a May sun in the hottest parts of the tropics. No; everything down to the cartridges and the lining of the coat pockets, in which most people carry them, should be carefully looked to, and no inefficiency tolerated for the sake of economy.

Expenses such as the above can, of course, be reckoned upon before starting, but there are others of a less certain nature. Occasionally beaters are killed, and then the compensation paid to their families is often heavy. Or an elephant may be sacrificed, and then you would be expected to pay for him! But these are dismal considerations, and apt, perhaps, to damp the rising ardour! Still, if they are ever to be glanced at, surely it should be before we start on our wild career. Whatever may happen afterwards must be considered as part of the enjoyment, even if, like myself, we end in becoming crippled for life! As soon as I had made up my mind that the game was really worth the candle, I sent to Messrs. Purdey for a twelve-bore gun, and a sixteen-bore rifle. Whilst they were *en route* I was so fortunate as to secure an invitation to join a large shooting party, so that when they arrived they were warmly welcomed. Up to this time I had cared so little for shooting that I had been quite satisfied with my excellent muzzle-loading guns, and was consequently quite ignorant of breech-loaders. But the friend with whom I was living kindly instructed me, and my faithful henchman, Mahomed Barker, aged about fifteen, in the art of putting them together, and loading the cartridges. I loaded twelve with my own hands, to show that I had really learnt the lesson, and these were the only ones I ever made up in my life. I mention this circumstance, as the sequel will show that native Indians are to be found who are more competent to perform such irksome duties than some Englishmen. Doubtless, as a rule, Orientals are careless and inconsequent to a degree that may be either amusing or appalling, according to the interests at issue. My advice, therefore, is to give whatever pay is necessary to secure a really good gun-bearer, and then leave everything, as much as possible, to him. He should be a Mohammedan, so that when there is no sport going on, he can wait at table, and do anything else that may be required. Men who can be thoroughly relied upon in every situation are rare in all countries, but they are to be found even amongst the natives of India.

Details such as the above may be uninteresting to the majority of readers; but as my object is, whilst amusing the many, to try and be of some use to a few, I shall continue, from time to time, to mention such incidents, and offer such advice as may be of some benefit to those who, like myself, aspire to a little amusement in the great jungles of India.

Perhaps I may as well here explain the usual method of

organizing a big-game shooting party. In all parts of India that I know of, except the Terai, the start is made early in April. Preparations should therefore be commenced in January. Either one proclaims oneself leader, and asks one or two friends to join, or one can join some one else's party. The country to be hunted is first decided upon, and then the leader opens communications with the chief native tracker (called a shikarrie) of those districts, which may extend to, say, one hundred miles by fifty. If the chief native hunter is already engaged, it is most advisable to try another locality altogether. Hence the necessity for getting everything ready in January, or even earlier. Government also lends elephants for the use of these parties. One should therefore lose no time in securing good ones before they have been promised to some one else. These animals vary greatly in their sporting qualities. Some are so game they will rush to the encounter with ardour, and join in mortal combat with the wounded and infuriated tiger; others will stand calmly till the day when they get actually mauled, and then absolutely refuse to have anything more to do with tigers for the rest of their lives.

Female elephants are often of this type.

The greater number of both sexes that one may see standing in the Government yards are non-combatants, who prefer the daily round of road-making, and other labour of a peaceful, or even domestic nature (such as minding the keeper's children), to adventures in the primeval forest.

All are extraordinarily intelligent. The mahouts, who live with them, are firmly convinced, not only that they understand all that is said in their presence, but that they can even tell if their keepers have stolen any portion of the flour allowed for their daily ration of cakes. This belief is so well established, that dishonest attendants always make up the right number of cakes, and get what they can of the flour by reducing their weight. It will be seen by and by that it does not answer to take them into the jungle under pretence of getting their forage whilst beating for tigers is really the object. They will soon find this out, and work dire confusion. Enquiries, therefore, have to be made as to the characters of the different animals available, and suitable ones applied for by their names. For most countries two good ones are sufficient, as they are only used when a wounded tiger takes refuge in very dense cover, and to carry the dead game into camp to be skinned. They are, very properly, not allowed to carry any luggage for the party. This is done by camels hired for the purpose. A good shikarrie, and suitable elephants, are the things which require the most forethought, as there are so many people to be consulted before they can be got ready. But there are some minor preparations which, though almost equally necessary, are often overlooked or despised on account of their simplicity.

Each sportsman should be provided with—

1. A small thong-bound ladder, eight feet long, composed of hollow bamboos.
2. A stout, hard-stuffed leather cushion, with a long strap and buckle sewn on to it, to fix on to the branches of trees.
3. Three or four hollow bamboo sticks, each about a yard long, strong enough to stand upon, and strings run

through each end to wind round the branches of trees to form a platform.

4. A leather water bag for drinking purposes.
5. A pair of dog-skin gloves, with half the fingers cut off, which, if you do not eventually require them, will not add much to your baggage. These will enable you to clasp the barrels of your gun when heated by the sun.

The whole of these things, together with a spare gun, can easily be carried by one man the short distance there is to be traversed between the rendezvous and your 'mool,' as the place you are to shoot from is called. I have sometimes been laughed at for providing myself with the above-mentioned little plant, but I have not minded this, as the scoffer has, in every instance, borrowed them of me, greatly to my own inconvenience!

Of course, you must get up trees when tiger-shooting, and be thankful when there are any. If you have immense courage, with a little patience you will certainly come to situations where you can display it all. It often happens that there are no trees, or other safe places whence to take the first shot; and even when there are, the tiger is frequently only wounded, and may have to be followed over ground where an elephant (if you have one) is unable to proceed. Then is the time to dismount, and lead the way, or even go alone through the cover in pursuit. Doubtless, tiger-shooting is a well-worn subject, and has been duly chronicled by men who are much abler than myself with both gun and pen. Yet I do not despair of throwing some new light on the sport, especially as regards the working of the elephants, in which few, if any, I think, have taken as much interest as myself. At all events, I have never heard of any one besides myself who cared enough for them to take upon himself the duties of mahout, by driving them in pursuit of the wounded tigers, and shooting the quarry, when come up with, from between the ears of the elephant, as I have done on many occasions. Of course, before venturing on the personal management of these animals, I studied their habits, and learnt all I could of them, as well from actual observation as by conversing with their keepers, whenever opportunity offered. It was also necessary that the people I went out with should be persuaded that I was equal to the task of elephant-driving, or they would by no means have consented to risk these valuable beasts to my unknown powers of managing them. My friends were even anxious lest I should come to grief and confusion in taking unknown responsibilities on myself. As to purchasing and keeping an elephant of my own, that was quite out of the question, as I could have no use whatever for him during ten months of the year, and even for the remaining two I could not be certain of getting leave to make a shooting trip.

Eventually, I overcame all my little difficulties, and found myself temporary master of one or more fine elephants, but not till some time had elapsed, and I had been obliged, during my first expedition of two months' duration, to be satisfied with a place in the howdah. As time rolled on, I made many prolonged excursions accompanied by these wonderful creatures, and bestowed a great deal of attention upon them. If I can only do justice to them in the present volume, I am sure my readers cannot fail to admire their great intelligence, docility, and superior general character. When, in addition to all their other fine qualities, they are endowed with a high-mettled courage, they are, in my opinion, next to man in the animal kingdom.

I will now conclude this first chapter by reminding the reader of what I have already once stated, namely, that this work is true in every particular, excepting, of course, the names of such friends and acquaintances as, in the course of my story, I may find myself obliged to mention.

I can lay no claims to distinguished authorship, and can only commend my narrative to the reader's kind indulgence on the score of its perfect veracity and genuineness.

CHAPTER II.

IN the month of April 18—, I was invited to form one of a large tiger-shooting party in Central India. For the first ten days we numbered seven, and after that five guns. This is considered a large party for tiger-shooting. We had with us four elephants—two large tuskers and two females, as far as I can recollect. They had all characters for staunchness. But the tusker, Bahadur Guj, was the only one who was really up to the mark. He was ready to face a tiger again after being mauled, and this, in my opinion, is the test of a good elephant. As might be expected, he had a queer temper, but still he was manageable. At this time he was eighty-two years of age, and had only killed two people (natives) in all that time. Considering the culpable carelessness of Orientals, it is to be wondered at that more were not sacrificed during so many years.

Having arrived at our first halting ground, we were all placed in position, and a beat commenced. The elephants formed part of the line of beaters, and were rallying points for them.

Unfortunately, they advanced too much in front of the men, so that when the latter put up the tiger, he tried to break through them instead of going on. He was thus surrounded by the beaters. I saw him rise up on his hind legs, and take the head of one of them in his mouth. In an instant he dropped his victim, and made some short pounces at the others, who (as one may suppose) were flying wildly in all directions. Numbers of them left the long cloths they wear round their heads sticking to the thorny bushes. This, it seemed to me, the tiger mistook for some snare, as he suddenly turned and bounded away at tremendous speed under the very tree I was in. Owing to the great pace he was going, I missed him. I have since seen others miss under the same circumstances, but at the time I felt my position keenly, being under the impression that other persons invariably dropped their tigers whenever and wherever they might get a glimpse of them.

It only remained now to follow up the tiger with the elephants. Owing to the fierceness of the sun, he would not like to travel far, or make many moves; at least so we hoped. After tracking for about an hour, he did turn out in front of one of the elephants, and was fired at by the people in the howdah, with what success I do not remember. For a moment he pulled himself up, and seemed about to charge, but he thought better of it, and was soon out of sight again. We followed him for some hours along the rocky banks of the river, visiting all the most likely nooks and corners, in hopes that he might have found it impossible to travel any farther over the burning rocks. Towards evening, however, he was descried at a distance of a quarter of a mile swimming across a deep pool that led into an extensive piece of forest. Here it was deemed advisable to leave him for the night, and organize a fresh plan for the morrow. Accordingly the next morning a beat was commenced from the opposite side of the wood, which proved successful. The tiger broke readily, and was shot by one of the party. It was a very fine male, in the prime of life. At first I wondered why it was so certainly to be considered the tiger of the day before. On asking the question, his feet were pointed out to me. They were completely raw with his long ramble over the burning rocks. It is not improbable that had he been only slightly driven, he would have travelled miles away during the night, and we might thus have lost him. Perseverance is often rewarded even when following up an unwounded tiger. It must not be supposed that the wounded beater was forgotten all this time. Of course he was borne from the field on the back of an elephant. As he passed me, I noticed his condition was more hysterical than prostrate. On his arrival in camp, his wounds were found to be much less serious than might have been expected. The human skull is often very hard, and the tiger, not having been wounded or much irritated, perhaps did not put forth all his strength. At any rate, the man recovered, and was presented with ten pounds. With this sum I was told he had set up as the banker of his village, that he developed a talent for compound interest, and became so rich that not all the persuasions of his clients could induce him to go out tiger-hunting any more. I do not vouch for the truth of the above; I only heard that it was so.

An occasional accident of this sort should not be looked upon as a proof of the brutal indifference of the English in India as to the lives of the suffering natives—quite the contrary. The natives, except under European leadership, will not go out against dangerous animals. Bapoo says, 'My cow is not killed, and besides I have obtained a charm from a holy man, by which she is made safe against tigers. Why should *I* go out?' On the other hand, Luximon says, 'My cow *is* killed; I shall certainly not go.'

The result is that the tigers get the better of the natives, and kill so many of them and their cattle, that I have seen many ruined villages, which have been abandoned owing to the neighbourhood of these animals. It is therefore a very good thing for the inhabitants when a well-appointed shooting party arrives. The whole population turns out, and every one, as far as possible, is provided with some rough instrument for making a noise. With these and their own voices, sufficient din is generally created to start whatever animals there may be in the jungle, long before the line of beaters comes up. At the first shot they understand that they are at once to make for places of safety till further orders. In this way accidents rarely occur, and, when they do happen, the sufferer or his surviving family are always fully compensated. Besides this, all the beaters are paid by the day, and each receives a gratuity if a tiger is killed. Thus there is much feasting in the villages where the party halts.

An ordinary beater in most districts receives from three to four pence a day when the beats have been blank, and double that amount when there has keen a kill. There will generally be about fifty or sixty of them. Their leaders will receive double the above sums. It is, however, unnecessary to enter into these details, as it is not likely any one would start for his first trip without an experienced friend to keep him straight. It is generally reckoned that tiger-shooting costs each man one hundred pounds per month. This includes his own living, keep of horses, and all other expenses.

One of the most curious features of tiger-shooting is the extraordinary tenacity with which both the Europeans and natives engaged in the sport adhere to certain traditions. In vain does the tiger break through the established rules before the very eyes of all engaged; the shikarries, both white and black, continue as firm as ever in their articles of faith, and, by their blind belief in the same, often lose a tiger. I propose therefore to mention a few of the most cherished laws, and to show in the following pages that they are in every instance fallacies—

(1) A tiger never charges unless wounded, or in defence of its young cubs. (2) It never lies up for the day in hot weather in a jungle where there is no water. (3) It never looks upwards so as to see any one in a tree.

I have already given one instance of an unwounded tiger charging, and nearly killing a beater, and I now propose to show how another was unprincipled enough to break two of the three rules at the same time.

A few days after the events narrated in the preceding chapter, I and the four others composing the party were duly posted across a wide nullah. Gibbon was told off for a tree growing on the top of the bank. The fork into which he climbed must have been quite twelve feet from the ground, so that as I sat in my bush in the bed of the nullah, he appeared almost in another world. As soon as we were all settled, the beat began. Our band on this occasion was unusually good. It produced a loud and piercing discord.

Almost immediately was heard the sound as of a horse galloping down the stony bed of the nullah. It was a tigress charging at full speed. Like a flash of lightning, she had cleared all obstacles, and was in the first fork of Gibbon's tree eight feet from the ground, and perpendicular to it. Gibbon fired down on her, and she fell to the earth with her jaw broken, but instantly charged again to the same spot, when another sportsman hit her with an express bullet in the back, making a fearful wound. On this she dropped into the brushwood, and made off.

The pursuit on elephants now commenced. There were three of them, and each had a line of its own to investigate. One called Bahadur Guj was much the staunchest, and knew what it was to be clawed.

Just as this elephant was passing a thick spot, the wounded tigress sprang upon his head. There was a brief but exciting struggle. Bahadur Guj got his enemy down, trampled it to death, and then flung its body upwards on to the bank of the nullah. I was unfortunately on another elephant, and did not see this final act, though I was close enough to hear the snorting and scuffling of the combatants. Fortunately for the elephant, the tiger's jaw was broken, so he received no injuries worth mentioning.

Seeing the position of the mahout on this occasion, I was resolved that sooner or later I would drive the elephant myself; but I was not able to do so during this trip, as the rest of the party had, I fear, but little confidence in me.

The next place we went to was called Rutlai. I was promised beforehand that here the tigers would be heard roaring in orthodox style. Also that none would probably be seen, as they always, at this place, seemed to elude the beaters.

The first prediction was amply verified, for immediately on arriving in the jungle the loud and deep tones of these usually silent animals were heard rolling magnificently down the valley. Their voices sounded quite close to us, but I was assured they were more than a mile distant.

It struck me as strange that the tigers in this jungle could be counted upon for vocal effects, whilst elsewhere they were mute, or nearly so. However, such certainly seemed to be the case. As regards their never appearing even before the most skilful beat, I think they probably had plenty of underground accommodation, and were able to conceal themselves effectually on the first sound of alarm. At any rate, if, as I believe, none were ever killed, they would get into regular habits, and always do the same thing. We had not time to stay long enough to study their customs minutely. On this occasion the beaters arrived at our posts having effected nothing but a cessation of the roaring. All was silent, and we were preparing for a move, when a beater ran up, and said he had seen the tail of a tiger in a thick corinda bush. Accompanied by a well-known Sikh sportsman called Gumbeer Singh, I followed the man to the bush, and looked in. In the centre of the bush we both plainly saw the hind quarters of a recumbent tiger. I asked him if he felt quite sure of what he saw. His answer was yes, and he raised his rifle to fire at it. This I would not allow, as it would have been a mistake to fire at the hind leg. We therefore retired, and reported what we had seen. We were not altogether believed, but still the bush was fired into from a little distance off, and fireworks were freely used. Nothing, however, came out, so Gibbon went with me, and we looked into the bush together. No tiger was visible, but, on the spot where it had been, sat a very young cub moving its head about in a bewildered manner in front of a black hole in the ground. This young animal was pronounced by the rest of the party to be an infant hyæna, but in my opinion it was a young tiger, and I offered to drive Bahadur Guj into the thicket, and make him clear the mouth of the hole. This, however, could not be done, as this great personage had taken himself off out of the jungle for the rest of that day. It seems that some years previously he had been nearly burnt to death in his stables. On that occasion he burst through the flames, and retreated many miles into the forest, whence he was only recovered after a long absence. Since then he could not abide the glare and smell of fireworks, and would not stay where they were being used.

Finally, a porcupine was seen to run into this very bush, and then the idea of a tiger being there was quite given up. But wrongly I think, as I have since seen many instances of the most unlikely animals living together. And this is particularly the case where porcupines are concerned, as they are the great excavators, and their diggings are much favoured by other animals, who in return for a home often tolerate the original incumbents.

CHAPTER III.

NO doubt the success of every undertaking in life depends greatly on the care and attention bestowed on what may be described as preliminary trifles. This is especially true with regard to tiger-shooting in India. No omission at the start can be rectified during the remainder of that trip. One of the most important of these minor considerations is a suitable costume. Not a scrap of white, not even the edge of one's pocket-handkerchief should be suffered to appear, as nothing attracts the eye in jungle scenes so much as white linen. The hat is quite the principal article of the toilet. As mine on three striking occasions saved my life, I propose to give a description of it.

The foundation consisted of a 'regulation helmet' with the full allowance of brim. On this was fixed a well-wadded and somewhat projecting cover. Inside and loosely secured to the ventilator by a string, was a wet sponge. A chin strap completed the edifice. Crowned with such a structure, even the most highly organized brain of a competition-walla may be expected to escape sunstroke in the hottest districts. On one occasion when at a place called Rutlai, the branch of the tree on which I was sitting broke, and I was seen to fall a distance of at least eight feet right on to my head. The ground was as hard as iron, and a friend who saw the catastrophe thought my neck must be broken. So far from this, however, I did not even feel any shock, nor did I receive the slightest bruise. I simply got up and proceeded to the next beat. No tiger appeared, but one of the party shot a fine bear. It presented a strangely heaving appearance as it lay upon the ground, and weak, small cries seemed to proceed from it. A nearer inspection revealed two little baby-bears hiding among the long fur of their dead mother. The poor little things clung convulsively to her, and were with difficulty torn from her side. Thus ended their last walk abroad, for both being wounded they had to be destroyed. The next animal we killed during this trip was again a bear. After a good deal of difficulty it was induced to bolt from its cave. This it did at great speed. On the first bullet striking him, he flew at the nearest object, which happened luckily to be a tree. This he embraced and mauled with great fury, till another shot killed him. This conduct on the part of the bear was not singular. When two are close together, and one is hit, it will often fly furiously at its companion, thinking it the aggressor. A fierce combat ensues, during which both may be shot.

I think that for big-game shooting the best weapon is a good smooth twelve-bore gun regulated to carry a bullet. A plain round ball, I also think, is the best missile when everything is taken into consideration.

Such weapons, when obtained of really first-rate makers, are true to something over the distance at which nine times out of ten one has to fire in the thick forests, where alone the larger animals are to be found. Two exactly similar guns of this sort are what I would recommend, as it is important that all the ammunition you may have about you should fit whichever weapon you may have in your hand.

On one occasion, at about this time, I was safely posted in a tree at the foot of a hill, and my friends were successfully concealed in the same way, forming an upward line to my right. In due time a magnificent bearded tiger came slowly prowling along the heights above us. It was quite a hundred yards from me, and as I was the farthest of all the party from it, it seemed not only madness for me to fire at it with a smooth-bore gun, but to do so under the circumstances was contrary to the very necessary rule, that the man nearest to whom a tiger breaks is to take the first shot. Without some such regulation, it is found that every one fires at once, before the tiger has had time to get within range, and many animals are thus lost. Unfortunately every one was so completely out of sight that they really were quite out of mind too. A favouring branch formed such a perfect rest for my gun, that for this one occasion at any rate my shooting was bound to be good. The bead seemed as though glued to the tiger. I fired! Eley's best green cartridge failed to go off! I pulled the other trigger, and hit the tiger well behind the shoulder. For an instant it clutched the narrow path on which it was proceeding, then, pulling itself together, it endeavoured to resume its way, when I gave it another bullet almost in the same place. This I think shows that a good smooth-bore may be depended upon even for what are considered long shots in big jungles. After receiving the contents of the second barrel, the tiger half charged, half rolled down the steep declivity, with such rapidity that the eye could not follow him. I mounted an elephant with a friend, and began to look about for him. At last he was discovered within a few feet of us, lying quite flat, with his head between two stones, thus making a good hiding-place out of almost nothing. He was not dead, but had his large bright eyes fixed upon us. We had just time to give him another shot or two, when another tiger was announced. We hurried in the direction indicated, but found nothing. On returning to pick up the dead tiger, he was nowhere to be seen, and was not found till after a considerable search. Although all his wounds were mortal, he had contrived to travel a hundred yards or so. Such and similar cases I ascribe to animals being endowed with more than the average vitality.

When all was over I had to meet the remonstrances of my friends on the subject of etiquette. Fortunately extenuating circumstances were found, and I was let down easily.

This, however, did not soften me towards my gun-bearer, Mahomed Barker, whom I considered worthy of little less than death for supplying me with a cartridge which examination proved to have been made up without a cap. He was, however, equal to the occasion. Taking a cartridge out of his own pocket, he pointed to a spot on it, and said, 'This is my private mark, the bad one belongs to the dozen you made up yourself.' It was even so. This proved a blessing in disguise, as I have never made up a cartridge since, thus saving myself an infinity of drudgery.

Whilst in the neighbourhood of a place called Chobara we saw a good many tigers. Most of them were very wild, and generally appeared going at full speed among the trees and underwood. Under these circumstances, I must say I have generally seen the tiger missed.

There is no doubt that in jungles that are beaten every season, the animals get to know something of the *modus operandi*, and shape their actions accordingly, thus becoming more and more difficult to kill. Nevertheless, in the above-named neighbourhood we got several. One of them disappeared, wounded, into the jungle. We searched everywhere, on the elephants, for it. At last we drew up in despair, and began to wonder what we should do next. Whilst standing there the elephant, Bahadur Guj, seemed uncomfortable, and kept rubbing one foot on the hard ground. The mahout said he had a thorn in his foot. The elephant was made to lie down, and he dismounted to examine into the matter. The mahouts are generally wrong in their suggestions. No thorn or other injury to the foot was to be found, so the elephant rose, and all was got ready to proceed on our travels, when some one suddenly saw the tiger crouching in the centre of the nearest bush to us, not more than three yards distant. Bahadur Guj had no doubt winded him, and was trying to make us understand that there was danger. This was a very fine elephant, ten feet in height, and of high courage. I have heard of his running away from a panther, but this was not his usual character. On that occasion he must have had lowering kind of water to drink, or the mosquitoes may have kept him awake all night. Nothing quells the spirit so much as want of sleep.

No one, however, is perfect, and Bahadur Guj's really bad point was his temper. He was known to have killed two people, but then he really was ill at the time, so he was excused. At this time, however, he was quite well. Yet one morning he made a sudden rush at the keeper of a rival male elephant that we had with us. The unfortunate man fell between his tusks, but, eel-like, slipped from between them, and darting behind a large howdah, he disappeared among the trees. The elephant, however, thought the man was in the howdah, so he fell upon it, crushing it like a nut, and then pitched the debris over his head. After performing this exploit, he became quite serene, and was like a lamb in the hands of his own man. One peculiarity of elephants is, that when desirous of killing any one, they nearly always select as a victim their own or a rival's attendant. All the old tuskers that I have seen in captivity have killed one or two persons in the course of their career. They are subject to a sort of fever, during which it is highly dangerous to approach them. But the attack is never sudden, and there is ample time to place them securely before the disease assumes a serious aspect.

Fatal accidents are, I may say, invariably due to the exasperating carelessness of the men themselves: The Asiatic creed is that everything is pre-ordained by fate, and that consequently all precautions are merely vexatious and useless.

This is the mental attitude before an accident. After the misfortune there is always a terrible row. The sufferers, or their relations (having raised their voices to a scream), blame everybody but themselves. To hear them, one would think they were the apostles of long-sighted and minute prudence. I once found our mess-man weeping loudly over his empty money-box. Amongst other questions, I asked what sort of a lock he had put on the box. 'Oh,' he sobbed out, 'I never, never locked it! I trusted to Providence; this is my fate. If the Government will only exert itself and take trouble, I shall get it back. Otherwise I am ruined for life.'

Such being the bias of the native mind, one can only wonder that there are not more fatal accidents of all kinds.

Before leaving this village (Chobara), we shot two or three tigers. In one of the beats I had been placed on the stump of a tree overlooking a ravine, along the bottom of which the tiger was to come. It, however, came from behind me, and stood staring at me. My position was such that I had to fire from the left shoulder. This I had never tried to do on any other occasion, so I missed the animal. As, owing to the change of approach, I was on a level with it, it was just as well that it ran from instead of at me. Had it charged, I should have had very little chance; for even if one could hit the tiger between the eyes, the bullet might easily glance off, owing to the angle at which the head is presented on such occasions. I have twice seen bullets traverse round the head under the skin without injuring the skull.

From Chobara we went to a place called Magruda, where, in lieu of sport, we had a great 'kick up' amongst our own followers. A small boy having proved troublesome, two elephant keepers, instead of ascribing his ill-conduct to fate, and putting up quietly with it, simply ran him through with a spear. As the lad was not fatally injured, the offenders were only tied up and well flogged. They considered themselves innocent of all fault, but said they could do nothing, and must as usual submit to the brutality of their European oppressors. A few days after this, we arrived at a place called Cooria. The place consisted of only a few huts, at some distance from which there was a solitary well. One of our followers, on going to draw water at this spring, found a Hindoo lying insensible on the brink. He had a long and deep sword-cut across his skull, from the effects of which he expired without making any sign. We could discover nothing concerning the tragedy, and I do not suppose the constituted authorities were more successful in their inquiries than ourselves. My own opinion is that murder is frightfully common amongst the Indian population, and that wild animals, especially snakes, are made to account for many a black deed committed in remote districts far from all European control.

The following incidents, I think, will show what a mistake it is to suppose that tigers are never found except in the near neighbourhood of water during the hot months of the year. Whilst out with a party of four, in the middle of May, we beat unsuccessfully for a fine tigress that had killed a cow during the previous night. The beat was properly conducted, but no beast of prey appeared. A mile or two distant there was a very fine jungle, but it was decided that as there was no water, so there could be no tiger in it. We therefore thought it a good opportunity to organize a beat on behalf of all our native shikarries, in order that they might slay for themselves deer, pig, and such-like animals for their own eating.

Accordingly, we repaired to the desired locality, and scattered ourselves about without taking any of the usual precautions. Some of us helped in the beat, and some of the beaters converted themselves into shooters, and took up such positions as seemed good to them. Things were proceeding very pleasantly, when suddenly a shot was fired by one of the natives, and word was rapidly passed that he had aimed at a tiger, which had not fallen, but had gone on, up the ravine, towards the head of the jungle. No blood marks could be found, and the bullet was held to have missed. This was ultimately proved to be true. But at the moment I doubted it, as the man was an excellent shot, and the tiger had come out slowly just in front of him. If, under the circumstances, he missed through nervousness, it proves that being anywhere near a tiger, one should always be expecting to see him, and arrange accordingly. At all events, the tiger was gone, and I and my friend had to do our best to find him. The elephant, Bahadur Guj, was called up, and I and my companion stood up in front of the howdah while the native who had first fired at the animal occupied the back seat with his little son. For a long time our search was fruitless. We worked up to the head of the jungle without finding a vestige of the enemy. On our way back my coadjutor pointed to a thick corinda bush, and said, 'That is a likely bush.' I looked, and there was the tiger, or rather tigress, standing in the centre of it. We fired together. There was a roar, a scuffle, and a dense cloud of smoke, under cover of which the tigress disappeared, having only been seen by the small boy in the back seat. The cover consisted entirely of detached bushes, so we felt sure she could not have gone far. At last we observed a black hole flush with the ground. This we approached cautiously, and on peering down, saw the legs of a recumbent tiger. We threw stones in, but the animal never moved, and on getting a view of her head, my friend put a bullet through it. The three of us now got down into the den, and with much difficulty contrived to get the beast out without injuring the skin. We now despatched the natives on the elephant to claim the help of the rest of the party, setting to work at the same time to do what we could towards the skinning. After a long time the mahout returned on the elephant, with the information that the rest of the party had dispersed to their own homes. They were all quite gone, so the best plan seemed to be to try and get the tiger on to the back of the elephant, and carry it to the nearest village. We had almost succeeded in doing this, when the mahout unfortunately shouted out the native word 'lagao,' which means 'lay it on.' But it is also the word used to make the elephant attack anything. In a moment, though he was down on all-fours, he whizzed one immense hind foot round furiously. One turn of his huge club-like limb hurled the tiger from him, and another just missed my friend's back by his forming himself suddenly into a bow. Then with extraordinary agility the elephant was suddenly on his feet, off to a distance of twenty yards, then whisked round and came to bay, ready to charge anything. The elephant was now in a state dangerous to approach, and would certainly have nothing more to do in a peaceful way with that tiger. So there was nothing for it but to complete the skinning, and a terrible job it was under the burning sun of May. However, notwithstanding a total want of proper instruments, we accomplished the feat very well, and, of course, had no difficulty in placing the trophy in its new shape inside the howdah. On examining the body, only two wounds were found—one rather far back behind the shoulder, and another apparently through the head. I say apparently, as the bullet had traversed under the skin, and had gone in at one side and out at the other, without touching the skull.

I ought to have mentioned that there was every appearance of this tigress' domicile having been excavated originally by porcupines. Quite at the bottom of it was a round hole just large enough to admit such animals, and going on to unknown depths. The passage also appeared clear, and as if in constant use, so I think the porcupines and the tiger probably shared the same quarters, and were on terms of sufferance, if not of amity. I am aware that this view would be disallowed by most frequenters of the jungle, but I have personally observed many instances of hostile animals occupying the same ground, and getting more or less used to one another. Once, during a beat, I saw a large Sambur deer emerge from the jungle out of shot, and following close at her heels was a panther. I could watch them for a long time slowly treading a narrow path together. Again, during the very trip of which I am now writing, we all saw a quantity of alligators and large river turtles floating amicably together in the middle of the river Chumbool. My friends went forth to get a shot at them. Whilst they were stalking them, one of the alligators opened its jaws, and, without any apology, grasped a turtle about the size of a drawing-room table. This he managed to demolish without much fuss, or causing any extraordinary stir amongst the others.

The events above described all occurred during my first trip out tiger-shooting, and it was some time before I could get out for another serious expedition. If the reader be not tired of the subject, I shall relate my further adventures in the subsequent chapters.

CHAPTER IV.

WHILST stationed at a place called Mehidpore, I often went out after tigers and panthers. They were not very plentiful in the immediate neighbourhood, so that, as a general rule, one got nothing but a terrible grilling in return for one's exertions. Shooting in India, especially during the hot weather, is very different to what it is in a cold or temperate climate, in which merely to take exercise in the open air is to enjoy oneself. One day's exposure in India is enough, with most people, to cause every bit of exposed skin to turn purple, after which it all comes off in flakes. This sounds more painful than it really is, though it is far from pleasant. Of course it makes a person very hideous, but as men are supposed to have no vanity, that, naturally, does not matter. Being, as one is, on the verge of heat apoplexy the whole time, is more serious, for a man never thoroughly recovers from a sunstroke. It is therefore essential to avoid one. A really good solar hat, with a wet sponge loosely tied inside it, is, I think, a certain preventive. These being the conditions under which the start is made, the reader will perceive the necessity for success which most people feel when they make up their minds to go forth, and the rage they often give way to when no animal is even seen after a long and painful toil. Under such circumstances, I have known an ordinarily just and kind gentleman turn upon the natives and beat them. This should never be done, as it prevents them from bringing in news on future occasions. I believe they always sincerely think that the animal they speak of is certainly in the jungle. A native has no firmness. I never met with one who could not by 'nagging' be got to disbelieve the evidence of his own senses. This is strange, as no arguments can shake their faith in such things as fairies, demons, omens, and the like. The only plan, when information of big game is brought to you, is to start off at once and take your chance. This is what I and two or three friends did one day at the above-mentioned place, when news was brought in of a panther. From the description of the locality, we were inclined to think that the beast existed only in the imagination of the villagers. It occurred to us, however, that we should certainly not see any wild creature by simply maintaining a firm seat each under his respective punkah. With this reflection, we got gasping on to our ponies, and were guided, at a walking pace, to a village about ten miles distant. On our arrival, we found all the more enterprising of the inhabitants, to the number of about thirty males, of all ages, mustered outside the mud walls of the hamlet. These people at once took us to a barren hillside, which, besides being quite close to the village, and much frequented by people, had only a very limited amount of cover. The beat, however, was commenced in the usual way, and to our great surprise a panther broke, and was shot by one of the party. It proved to be a female, and was one of the two smallest I ever saw. I do not think it could have measured more than four feet from tip of nose to tip of tail, or have weighed more than forty pounds. Yet it was a most interesting specimen, for it had its life, evidently a most difficult one, registered upon its body. Its lower jaw had been so smashed that it could never, since the accident, have made any use of the long front teeth, with which these animals fix on to their prey. This misfortune must have occurred to it early in life, as even the scars were scarcely visible, and nature had worked wonderfully to repair the damage as far as might be. True, it had not attained to so much as half its proper size, yet it had lived, and, incredible as it may seem, contrived to kill not only goats, but also cattle. There before us was the calf it had killed the previous night, and which (till we killed the panther) we thought must have been worried to death by smaller animals, as there were none of the large fang marks which are always so conspicuous about the bodies of the victims of the larger beasts of prey. The panther about which I am now writing was killed almost instantaneously. There was nothing more to do than to hand it over at once to one of our own permanent followers, with a view to the skin being carefully taken off and brought into camp. Without this precaution, the head would have been deprived of the whiskers, which add so much to its appearance when set up. The natives have some superstition with regard to these bristles, and almost all of them, no matter to what caste they may belong, consider it a solemn duty to destroy them. One idea, I know, is that the least fragment of one will kill you, for on one occasion I pretended I was going to swallow a small piece, which caused several of them to rush at me, and actually to interpose by force to prevent what they thought would prove an act of suicide. I suffered myself to be overcome, as I thought that, owing to the stiff nature of the hair, and its serrated edges, it really might prove injurious.

Shortly after the death of this small panther, I was making an ordinary journey, which took me at the end of three days to the large and well-known city of Oogein. My tents were pitched just outside the town, and I was very glad to get in and away from the sun. I had just finished breakfast, when some excited natives came running up to inform me that there was a panther in one of their gardens, which had just mauled a man; and would I be so good as to go and shoot it? There was no jungle for miles round, so I thought this time the animal would surely turn out to be nothing more than a jungle cat or a savage dog. 'Well,' I said, 'where is the man who has been mauled, I will inspect his wounds?'

'Oh,' they answered, 'he is dead, quite dead. How can *he* come before your honour?'

On this I ordered my rifle to be got ready, and, followed by a constantly-increasing crowd of the most useless description of natives, I proceeded to the spot, or as they called it, the garden. Now a garden, in the ordinary native Indian sense of the word, is so different from what the same term implies in England, that I may as well describe this one. In the first place, there had never been a single flower in it, nor even any ornamental shrubs. Neither were there any paths, summer-houses, or other signs that beauty was intended. There was an unlovely field of hemp, of about half an acre in extent, surrounded by a thick, gnarled, and ill-used jasmine hedge, under the densely-matted branches of which even a tiger might have effectually concealed itself in lairs proof against all missiles thrown by the hand. In addition to this, the hemp itself formed a better cover than the finest crop of wheat would do in England.

At the corner of this field stood a magnificent mango tree, quite a forest giant, with dark-green leaves like those of a camellia. It bears a profusion of large golden fruit, of which the natives are very fond. It was doubtless this tree, and a few poor vegetables called bhendies and baiguns, that made this place a garden. Well, I took up a position at the corner of the hemp-field, and the natives endeavoured to drive the animal towards me by forming a line on the other side and advancing with deafening clamour and much throwing of stones. Nothing, however, showed, and a lull ensued, during which I bethought me to inquire for the corpse of the slain man. He was pointed out to me walking about among the beaters, much bandaged up, but not looking greatly the worse for the encounter. Just as I was going to examine his wounds, a cry rose of 'The panther! the panther!' I ran in the direction indicated, and there was the beast prowling off across a lately cut corn-field. I pursued, as I was a hundred yards distant, and I wished to get within thirty yards before firing; but without seeming to go any quicker, he always kept at that distance. I began to get out of breath, and was meditating a long unsteady shot, when I saw that he was heading for a narrow strip of standing corn. I thought he would lie up in this, so as soon as he entered it I made a last effort, and ran as hard as I could. Before, however, I got into this crop it emerged at the other side, as far off as ever, and with a few graceful slides and bounds, disappeared into some more standing grain. I was now quite breathless, and almost despaired of bagging this tantalizing brute. Under these circumstances, I naturally tried to throw the blame on somebody else, so I turned to my gun-bearer, named 'Chowpatty,' who was close at my heels with a spare weapon, and pointing to the distant crowd of Oogeinites, I said bitterly, 'If those idiots were only respectable "junglees," instead of a town rabble, they would stop their abominable noise, make a rapid detour, form a line a quarter of a mile off, and drive the panther on to us, who would be lying behind this haycock.' Chowpatty instantly communicated this harangue to the people in rear of us. To my great surprise they suddenly became a compact and silent body, flying off at great speed to the right, where they gained a nullah and vanished. Chowpatty and I flattened ourselves behind the haycock. In ten minutes we heard quite a grand beat coming towards us, and almost immediately the panther, which looked large and massive, appeared at a distance of twenty yards, standing still and staring hard at us. I fired, and hit its right foot. In its first moment of astonishment and sharp pain, it put its wounded toe up to its mouth. Fortunately, before it could form a second thought, my second bullet had gone through its heart, and it fell stone dead. Notwithstanding its fine appearance, it only measured six feet two inches as it lay on the ground. Its limbs were, however, unusually large and powerful; at the same time its teeth were very white, and not the full length, so I have no doubt it was a three part grown male, and would, in another year, have been a giant of his kind. This also would account for his being found in such unlikely quarters. During the monsoon months the forest is joined on to the town by an unbroken mass of grain crops, so thick and high as to afford a perfectly secure cover for any number of wild animals. I once measured a stalk of jowaree—the staple grain—and found it over thirteen feet in length. I purposely selected one that was of average length.

Now as all this cultivation was being gradually got in, this young panther, from want of experience, had probably retreated in the wrong direction, till at last he had decided to live in the hemp-field, with the jasmine hedge as a stronghold. In an evil hour he floored the native proprietor, on the very day when a European fond of shooting such beasts happened to be on the spot.

As soon as the shooting was over, I visited the said proprietor, and found him rather shaken after the excitement had worn off, so I gave him some brandy to drink, and mixed some with salt for him to put on his wounds, which were not serious, owing partly to the shortness of the panther's teeth, and partly to its not having attacked any joints. I heard soon afterwards that he had quite recovered.

During the whole of the period concerning which I have written so far, I was hoping some day to drive the elephant myself after the wounded tigers. This, it seemed to me, would be a pleasing novelty, and likely to lead to a variety of adventures. There was much, however, to be done before this idea could be carried into effect.

Firstly, I must be somewhere where I could borrow an elephant to practise upon. And this was not a difficult matter, for, owing to the number of officers who had been killed for want of the assistance of an elephant, Government, during the time I was in India, would lend their animals for this sport. This was, no doubt, a wise course, as the authorities wish to encourage tiger-shooting; and just at the time for it there happens to be no work, such as moving troops or road-making, for any of the beasts belonging to the public service; all, therefore, fits in very well in this respect.

Secondly, I had to consider how it would be possible to manage the elephant and my gun at the same time. This led to my inventing a most simple and excellent arrangement with two straps, by means of which, if I dropped the gun entirely, it just hung with the butt in the hollow of my right shoulder, ready to come up in an instant. The heavy driving-hook, called 'ankoos,' could be fastened by a cord of the required length round my waist, so that it also could be dropped without losing it. By these arrangements the driving and shooting weapons could be interchanged as rapidly as could possibly be desired, according to whether it were the elephant or the tiger that required tackling. Last, and most important of all, was a good chin-strap to my helmet. Tigers and elephants you may escape from, even when they are doing their worst, but to be under a May sun on the plains of Hindustan, with nothing on your head, would be certain death to any ordinary European.

Having mentally worked out all these notions, and a good many more, which would be too tedious to set down, I arrived at a place called Mhow. Here I found plenty of Government elephants, all for the moment idle. The officer in charge kindly allowed me the use of a fine lively young male whereon to learn the mahout's art. To make my first staff, I went to where the elephant was kept, and, having got on his back, I slid behind his ears. I now found out what a 'kellawar' was. It was a sort of necklace of cord and network mixed, fastened round the animal's throat, which could be tightened or loosened at pleasure. Into this the mahouts stick their toes, to help them to keep their seat when things are not going smoothly. As I wore boots, I had to have my feet pushed through this structure, which was then tied in a bow, which could be adjusted by the rider. The kellawar, when tight, is an instrument of torture. Imagine being stretched, as it were, across two horses, and then having your heels tied tightly together underneath them. Still, one can get accustomed to anything, and I decided that if I had to be killed, it should be on the elephant, and not off him. To this I adhered throughout my subsequent adventures, though I sometimes had to be taken off at the end of the chase, and then was unconscious of having any legs. They were so numbed on one occasion, that when put on the ground I felt as though I were supported miraculously in mid-air somewhere about the waist. However, I could see my legs, so I knew this was only fancy. Of course, the mahouts, being without shoes, can slip their feet in and out at pleasure, and thus have a much more comfortable time of it. After three or four lessons I became sufficiently expert to drive myself to the houses of my lady friends to indulge in the usual luxury of early morning tea. Under these circumstances, it was necessary to choose routes by which I should not meet people on horseback, as the equine race object strongly to passing an elephant on a narrow road.

Scarcely had I acquired the necessary proficiency in my new calling, when I induced some friends to allow me to join their shikar party, which was to start immediately from a place called Neemuch, about 160 miles distant. I made the best arrangements I could for this trying journey. The heat in that part of the world on the 1st of April would, I knew, be quite enough to kill me; but then one is always living through impossibilities, especially in India. I therefore paid a visit to the mail contractor, Mr. Ardasseer, and asked him what he could do for me. 'Oh! Sir,' he said, 'dismiss all thought. I can cause you to arrive the same as if you were sitting in your own bungalow. For the small sum of eighteen pounds I shall supply you with a bullock-carriage, in which you can recline on your bed, and sleep for three days and two nights, and find yourself at Neemuch, all like nothing. I have relays of bullocks posted every three miles. The footman, who will sit beside the driver, will only have to shout, and a fine pair of richly-caparisoned animals will be on the roadside before you have time to stop.' 'But,' I said, 'what about food? I can't sleep all that time without eating.' 'Why,' he said, 'the footman will get you milk out of the villages; and, besides, you will be able to take a hamper. My bullock-carts are so commodious, they will take everything you can desire.' Still, I objected that the same footman could hardly be on duty, perched on a small board, and going over deep ruts and large stones all the time. 'Not able to do it!' he exclaimed; 'what right has that wretched one to get tired? Do I not feed him? and is he not bound to obey my orders? Why, if I could only secure a return passenger, he should not sleep a wink till he got back to Mhow.' Such a discourse as the above would have inspired the most sceptical with some hope, so I fixed nine o'clock on the night of the 1st of April for the start. The day and the hour arrived, and with them the dreadful vehicle outside the mess-door. I said good-bye to the friend who came to see me off, and plunged headlong in. It was fearfully hot and close; feather beds had to take the place of springs, and it was long before exhaustion set in in lieu of sleep. No, it was never sleep; it was merely exchanging real for ideal misery. I fancied myself the victim of a superior power, which sometimes assumed the shape of a gridiron, and sometimes that of a poultice. When in possession of my senses I craved for wine or brandy—though I was determined to take none. Not a drop of anything passed my lips, except soda-water, tea, and tepid water taken from the fiery brooks; for it would never have done to make myself ill before even joining the party.

All the way from Mhow to Neemuch there were what are called dāk bungalows, kept up at the expense of Government. The traveller is charged two shillings a day for the use of the house, and there is usually a mess-man, who will supply all your wants on a contract of his own.

On this line, however, there was only a care-taker, called a puttewalla, whose caste, as I found on the one occasion that I stopped for shelter, was of such an exalted nature that he could not open a box of sardines for me. Under these circumstances, 'Forward' seemed the only watchword. There was no rest for the poor puttewalla (or footman) attached to the vehicle. The bullock-drivers were all right, as they were changed with the bullocks. Never once were the promised bullocks ready. During daylight I often saw the poor man, whose name was Luximon, flying over the fields towards a distant pair engaged in ploughing. Wild were the gesticulations of himself and the ploughman. Sometimes they would both disappear, apparently in quest of another pair, and be absent several hours. Once gone, how could I recapture the unhappy man? He came to me, and said, 'If only your highness' (hoozoor) 'would go with me, we should get the bullocks at once.'

I answered, 'Never! I would rather die in this cart than get out every three miles to do your work.'

At a place called Mundsor I was kept seven hours. It was night, and I suppose we all went to sleep; at any rate, I own I did.

When about half-way over the journey, you come to a large native town, called Rutlam. Here there is a rajah, who is supposed to be independent, only, of course, it would never answer to let him do anything he liked. He had just built a new palace, and one of his ministers took me over it, and was very civil. In the grounds was a fine aviary, with wire quite fine enough to keep the smallest birds from escaping; yet all the poor little creatures were hung round in small cages. When I explained to the minister that the birds ought to live at liberty within the handsome edifice, he looked stealthily at me, and said he would ask the political agent about it.

At last, after a period of three nights and two days, Neemuch was descried at daybreak. I stopped the cart, got out, and made a sort of toilet by the solitary roadside. I then walked into camp, and arrived at the quarters of my friend in time to rouse him from his slumbers, and enjoy an early cup of good tea in his company. His first words were, 'Why, how fresh you look!' This, reader, was my reward for resisting the constant desire I had had to indulge in strong drinks. To look well you must be well, and, of course, the latter is the most important point.

CHAPTER V.

HAVING arrived at Neemuch, I found that, owing to unforeseen circumstances, the shikar party would not be able to make a start for a week or ten days; therefore there was ample time for me to see what sort of elephants there were in the commissariat yard, and to try and get on to good terms with the one I might select for riding.

The superintending officer was very kind, and gave me all the information in his power. We went down to the lines together, and there, looming vast among five or six others, stood an immense tusk elephant, of handsome shape, and nearly ten feet high. 'That,' I said, 'is the elephant I should like to ride.' My friend at once said that I could do so, and proceeded to give me the history of the animal who was destined to play an important part in my adventures, and to die a tragic death. His name was Roghanath Guj, and he bore a very high character both for courage and gentleness. During a long career he was only known to have killed two people, who had fallen victims to their own carelessness in approaching him during the fever, which he always had during the rainy months from the beginning of June to the end of September. This disease always began gradually, and hitherto the patient had invariably been properly secured in time to prevent any one from being injured unless they chose to put themselves in his way. I was quite satisfied with this report; and early the next morning the mahout brought him up to my quarters. I began by feeding him with bread and sugar, whilst the keeper was explaining to me the animal's manners and customs. Though ever ready to obey orders, he much disliked having to kneel. An elephant's elbows are tender, and some get a diseased joint from being made constantly to assume this posture, on all sorts of ground, to enable people to mount. I began, therefore, by getting up in the orthodox style, which was as follows:—On standing before him, and indicating that you wished to mount, he would lower himself by advancing both his front legs; you then took hold of his lips at the root of the tusks, and placed a foot on the tip of each. He then rose to his full height, and tossed up his head as high as his short neck would allow, and so enabled you to slide between his ears. To dismount, he would half-stoop on one hind leg, and raise the other outwards. On to this extended limb I would slip by means of his tail, and from thence to the ground, which last was an easy step. To do all this with an elephant at the first interview was, naturally, rather risky; but as our acquaintance was to be short, I thought it advisable to pass a vote of confidence at once. I wished my first ride to be a pleasure to all concerned, especially to Roghanath Guj, as it was his first experience of an enlightened European mahout. The native man, from want of thought, keeps up a constant drumming on the beast's head with the goad, or 'ankus;' I therefore hoped not to use it at all. Such an improvement all at once, however, proved more than even the elephantine mind could grasp. He began really to enjoy himself, going his own way more than mine, till at last he marched straight into an immense forest tree of the banyan species, and commenced to browse. . He seized the boughs above his head, and, tugging violently at them, brought them down on my devoted skull. This was too much. I raised the ankus, and brought it down on his head with a blow that brought blood through the skin. This had the desired effect, and he at once bundled off by the road he knew I wanted him to go. He merely took with him a branch about the size of a small apple-tree to discuss as he went along. From this moment we were friends, and I do not think I ever had to use the hook again so as to bring blood; generally it was sufficient to tap him with my fingers to get him to do what I wanted.

The delay at Neemuch was in many respects advantageous, as it enabled me to get on to really familiar terms with my great ally, and also my servants had a good rest after their long trudge on foot from Mhow. By the time all was ready, a travelling photographer most opportunely appeared upon the scene. We all mustered to have our picture taken. There were five officers, one of whom was a doctor. Then there was the head jungle-shikarrie, called Peyma, an ancient and shrivelled chief, who had seen a fabulous number of tigers killed. On each side of him squatted one of his sons, whilst the centre of the group was formed by the mighty Guj with me on his neck, and his mahout, Ghassee Ram, standing by his side. Two other elephants were told off for our use, but they were not in the picture. One of them was quite young, and it was only expected to help in the beat, where it would be of much use. The other was a fine female called Mānut Dār. She had a high character for firmness in the presence of a wounded tiger. But she had never been mauled; it remained, therefore, to be seen what effect a personal encounter would have on her. A female elephant is almost always ruined by a tiger fixing on to her. It is therefore considered proper to pull up at some distance from where the tiger is lying up, and pelt him with stones or bullets, and then to shoot him as soon as he shows himself.

Such being the character of female elephants, I resolved on always riding a male, which, if it stands one mauling, will develope fierceness, and learn to charge furiously into any cover where it thinks the tiger may be. Even this is objected to by many people, as, owing to their limited field of vision, they get hurried and charge injudiciously. I heard of one who, catching a glimpse of something moving in a bush, at once made a rush. A little bird flew out, whilst its huge assailant fell over the precipice, on the edge of which the bush was growing, and was killed on the spot.

Owing to occasional instances of mistaken zeal, like the above, the charging elephant has been pronounced a mistake, and but few people will go out with them.

Perfection is represented by a gentle and steady female, who will stand quite still whilst the tiger is roaring and charging in all directions. Unfortunately this phlegm seldom survives the first mauling, after which the steady female almost always becomes wild with terror, whilst the fighting male learns to rush furiously into the fray. The latter is what I like, so I never drive one of the gentler sex except in the absence of a cross old tusker. A well-known steady female is worth—say in the Terai—from three to four hundred pounds. The price of a male is more uncertain, varying from fifty pounds to at least seven hundred, at which price I have seen one advertised for sale. The large elephants, if they are tolerably quiet, fetch large sums for purposes of state ceremonial. A rajah dearly loves to ride the 'high elephant' in a procession.

I have now quoted the market value of elephants, which is very different to the Government prices. The State animals are not for sale, so that if any are to be sold by auction, it is understood that there is some objection to them, and consequently they would seldom fetch more than a hundred pounds. When any are lent to you for shooting purposes, a printed form is handed over with each animal, stating his supposed age, his name, his height, and price. The latter is calculated at what he has cost the authorities to catch in one of their 'keddahs.' The highest figure that I ever met with in one of these official documents was one hundred pounds.

Our plan for the trip, concerning which I am now going to write, was to strike the camp when we moved, after breakfast, and to dine at the next halting-ground, doing our shooting *en route* between the two places.

This arrangement resulted in breakfasting between ten and eleven o'clock, under the partial shade of what was often a very shabby tree; for at this time of the year the burning sun, combined with drought, causes the leaves to fall. And in any case the heat at that hour was such that I had great difficulty in facing any kind of food.

For several days our labours met with no success, the tigers in that district not being so plentiful as we had expected.

About the end of the first week, however, we arrived at the Beria nullah, which contained a tigress. As all these large nullahs greatly resemble one another, a description of this one may amuse some of my readers. Marching perhaps for miles over a level plain, off which all the crops have been gathered, and on which nothing is now left but dried bushes and stones, you at last catch sight of some tops of trees evidently growing below an abrupt declivity. Suddenly you arrive on the brink, and find quite a new country spread out before you. The whole land is deeply scarred and gashed with watercourses. The banks may be three or four hundred feet high, and the width from one to the other anything from twenty yards to a quarter of a mile. The character of the whole of this extensive tract is rugged in the extreme. Distance, of course, harmonizes the view, but when near, all seems to have sprung from chaos. Huge forest trees give place to vaster rocks, forming often a solid wall, black in colour, and hundreds of feet high. Such masses only occur at intervals. The usual nature of the slopes may be described as one continued land-slip, where rocks great and small lie one on another from top to bottom of the ascent. The interstices are filled with thorny brushwood, cactus, and large trees, wherever the soil admits of their growth.

In the centre of the valleys there is always at least a chain of deep, clear pools of water, and sometimes a rushing but unequal stream flows on to the nearest great river, perhaps five hundred miles off.

Sometimes a width of twenty miles of country by five hundred in length, will be torn by a system of nullahs, such as I have attempted to describe, all apparently in direst confusion, but which a bird's-eye view or a map would show to be all tending to one common end in some mighty river, on their way to which they pass through many large forests. Between these nullahs the land is level, and of rich quality. Consequently villages abound, and the inhabitants keep cattle and flocks in considerable numbers. Now, domestic animals being so much easier to circumvent than wild ones, numbers of tigers and panthers quit the remote forests, and, attracted by the flocks and herds, take up their abode among the nullahs, where they afford excellent sport to any one fond of big-game shooting.

The dry months of April, May, and sometimes the early part of June, must be selected for the work. Early in June the monsoon, a sort of deluge, sets in, when the country becomes impassable. This lasts till the end of September, by which time, owing to the combined growth of crops and wild cover, it becomes impossible to stir an inch off the roads and footpaths. In addition to this, water being plentiful in all directions, it is impossible to say where the tiger is likely to lie up after he has gorged himself with a heavy meal of beef. The tiger seldom kills sheep or goats. These he leaves, as a rule, for panthers, who greedily avail themselves of the privilege. In many parts of India it is customary to tie up young domestic bull-buffaloes near all the favourite drinking-places of the tiger. These are visited early in the morning, being viewed, if possible, from such a distance as not to disturb the tiger, who, should he have dined off one, is sure at this time of the year to be reposing in some shady retreat close at hand. If not interfered with, he will always feed on what he has killed himself till it is all eaten, no matter how bad it may get. Unfortunately, when one takes to man-eating, the relations of the victim will never allow the remains to continue on the ground, so that the brute may be killed whilst making his second repast. If the people could overcome their repugnance on this head, the list of victims would often be much shorter.

It was not the custom in the part of the country about which I am now writing to tie up anything. We merely had a succession of beats for twelve or fifteen miles,—the distance from one camping ground to another. Our first successful beat was, as I have already stated, at the Beria ravine. We had just finished a blank beat early in the day, and were all making our way on foot among all the cover, when some beaters viewed the tigress. Intense excitement now took the place of that apathy into which we were fast sinking for want of success. No one knew exactly where the animal had gone, but the aged Peyma, who was acquainted with every inch of the ground, had his suspicions, according to which he placed us in fresh positions, and organized another beat. The forest trees were scaled at suitable points by scouts, and before long some of these saw the tigress enter a cave which was well known to our native Indians. This was on the side of a very steep, cramped, and thickly-wooded ravine, into which Peyma and his sons said it would not be fair to send the beaters.

I was now asked if I would drive the elephant up to the stronghold. This I eagerly consented to do, and I hurried up on to the plain to look for him. There he stood with his companion, Mānut Dār, out in the open, where the mirage magnified and distorted them into monstrous-looking creatures, which might, by any one fresh from England, have been mistaken for hills undergoing an earthquake. I rushed up to Roghanath Guj, and never shall I forget the pleasure with which I felt myself on the end of his tusks, and being wafted on to his head. Peyma got into the howdah which was carried by the female elephant. Thus accompanied, I led the way down the rugged side of the ravine, and entered the brook which was running at the bottom of it. I turned down stream, and before long found the way barred by the sweeping branch of a large banyan tree. I ordered the elephant to tear this down, which he did at once with his trunk. The falling of the bough was like drawing a curtain. There sat the tigress, just above me, at the mouth of her den, seemingly awaiting events. I at once fired at her, when she disappeared, and the natives in the trees all called out that she was about to spring on me. In vain did the veteran Peyma try to bring up his elephant to my support. The mahout, when jeered at from above, said nothing would make her advance another inch. At the first outcry, accompanied by some short roars from the tigress, even the mighty Guj turned his back to the foe. But I think he did this thinking I might like it, for I had no difficulty in wheeling him round and urging him up to the mouth of the cave. In the meantime the tigress had taken an upward course, and had received a bullet in her leg from some one posted above. This caused her to rush into the cave again by a back entrance just as I arrived at the front one. She glared at me for an instant, but before she had time to spring I despatched her with a bullet through the chest. I was much pleased with this adventure, as it was my first effort on the neck of the elephant, though not the last or the most exciting.

The nullahs in this part of the country were usually well stocked with tigers and panthers, so before shifting our ground we were determined to beat them thoroughly. On one occasion a panther was just escaping over the Gātie ravine, when one of the party made a very good shot with his rifle, killing the animal at once. It rolled itself from top to bottom of the precipice, and expired without, as far as I remember, giving any more trouble.

We measured him as he lay on the ground, and found him to be eight feet from tip of nose to tip of tail. I have seen a full-grown tigress not measure much more, but her weight would probably be double that of the largest panther. The latter have longer tails, and run generally more to length than tigers. For the benefit of such of my readers as may be interested in estimating the size of the animals about which they are reading, I would state that there are three methods of measurement.

1. Measuring the skin when stretched out on the ground. By this plan you can make your tigers any length you like, as the skin can be drawn out to the most unnatural dimensions.

2. Some people make a mark on the ground near the animal's nose, and another at the tip of the tail. They then remove the animal, and measure the intervening space. The objection to this method is, that if an animal has to be carried a long distance before being measured, it becomes stiffened into a doubled-up posture, by which it is much shortened.

3. The third, and I think fairest plan, is to run the tape along the animal from his nose, between the ears, and along the spine to the end of the tail. This, at any rate, is how I always measured my big game. Taking their weight would be most interesting, but I never could make up my mind to carry the necessary load of scales, etc. The spring-balance would not be satisfactory, as it would be liable to get out of order, thus rendering the statistics untrustworthy.

Carnivorous beasts are often very unpleasant to skin,—some much more so than others. The panther above referred to was quite the worst I ever met with in this respect. I found it impossible to go near him. Even the natives, whose experience in this respect was so much greater than mine, and who, in consequencc, could face almost any effluvia, were severely taxed, but still they struggled manfully with their feelings till they got the handsome skin off. The body was then exposed for the vultures and kites to dispose of. Not one, however, would go near it. In all my experience I have only twice seen these voracious scavengers act in this way. The circumstances were all similar on both occasions, so that it would seem as though they had some instinct to warn them off the remains of certain apparently quite healthy animals.

The next place we came to was called Rajgurh. Here we all lodged in the deserted and partially-ruined palace of an ancient race of Indian princes. Though it had probably never been a very sumptuous structure, yet it was still very beautiful and spacious. The principal feature was a clear and deep sheet of water enclosed within its precincts, and called a tank. This was built all round with ten or twelve steps of masonry forming a square, the sides of which looked about eighty yards in length. These steps terminated in a smooth plinth, also of stone, and thirty or forty feet in width. On to this plinth the apartments opened. Here during the long moonlight nights would the ladies of the harem disport themselves, after the burning heat of the day. Sometimes they would recline on cushions whilst the nautch girls showed their grace, or the professional story-teller would hold their simple minds enthralled with one of his never-failing romances.

The figure of the square was not regular; the buildings had been run out in places so as to enclose gigantic banyan trees, under which tasteful summer-houses had been erected. The buildings, however, were all connected right round the tank, so as to ensure perfect privacy. From the outside, as one approached, nothing was visible but dark, forbidding walls without any aperture except the principal gate, through which we were to enter. As the country around was exceedingly rough and dry, it may be imagined what a refreshing change it was to get into this little paradise, even in the days of its decadence.

Quitting this pleasant retreat, we entered the tiger jungle under the blaze of a mid-day sun. The chief native shikarries led the way on the elephants, we followed on horseback, and finally came the beaters, forming a long and straggling 'queue.' Suddenly there was a stoppage at the head of the procession. I hurried to the front to ascertain the cause, The elephants, leading horsemen, and many followers were all standing over a strange-looking little object waving about on the ground, for all the world like a couple of white pocket-handkerchiefs agitated by the wind. This proved to be one of the common Indian plovers, known from their peculiar cry as 'Did-you-do-it,' sitting on her two precious eggs, and defending them with her life against the uplifted foot of the elephant. The poor little bird had bent her long slim neck so as to place her head between the two eggs, and thus shut out from view the dreadful dangers that surrounded her. In this position, she flapped her white-tipped wings in hopes of mercy. Need I say that such noble devotion was duly appreciated! We continued our march, leaving a trustworthy native standing over her to warn off any evil-minded or careless stragglers. The attention of all was soon called from this little episode by one of us taking a long shot at a panther. It made off through the jungle, but was apparently severely wounded, as it left a well-marked trail of blood on its tracks. We followed on foot, as we could go faster than the elephants, and, of course, we could only thus see the marks of the wounded animal. After going nearly a mile, we came to a very thick bush, in which we quite expected to find the panther, and in point of fact it had lain up there, and left quite a pool of blood to mark the spot. We felt much encouraged, and thought it could not be far off now. On we went, as fast as we could, without losing the tracks. This was, however, an instance of a cat having nine lives, for the blood drops gradually became less and less frequent, till at the end of another mile they ceased altogether, and nothing more was ever seen or heard of this panther, nor did we get anything whilst staying at this place.

About a week or ten days after the date when I shot the tigress from the neck of the elephant, information was brought to us that there was another tiger in that same ravine, and that its roaring was heard every night round the neighbouring villages, though no one had been able to see it.

We were at no great distance from the spot, and our arrival was so timed as to commence the beat early in the day, that is to say, at about eleven o'clock. All promised unusually well till we got to our ground. There, it was at once apparent from the long faces of our scouts, and the funereal pace at which they approached us, that something had gone wrong. Our wildest imaginings fell short of the reality. A sporting Indian royalty had pitched his tents under the very grove of trees which, on the principle that the jungle belongs to every one, we had naturally considered to be our own. For a moment no one could speak; we became as men paralyzed. Our gallant leader, Jones, was the first to rally, as in duty bound. Like the drowning man catching at a straw, he expressed a hope that this native dignitary had heard nothing of the adjacent tiger, and might be only on his travels in a general sort of way. 'Would it were thus,' groaned the aged Peyma, shaking his turbaned head. 'This thief,' thus he called him, 'has come here expressly to shoot our animal; he pretends to have heard nothing of the existence of this party, and, moreover, asserts that this jungle is in his territory, and that he is the lord of it. But I know positively that he is simply the enemy of the real rajah, and a liar from his birth. I know him of old, and will answer for it that if you order him to decamp at once, as an impostor, that he will never dare to make any complaint.' This discourse was all delivered under an isolated tree, and in the native tongue. We, the higher powers, now discussed the subject. We were inclined to believe all that our faithful follower had told us, and to take his advice. But, on the other hand, the claimant might not have been an impostor after all, and to turn a man out of his own property would be sure to lead to awkward complications. At last a very nice middle course was decided upon, as follows:—We would call upon the rajah, seem glad to see him, and propose as a great treat that he should ride in the howdah on the back of Mānut Dār, and, together with all his armed followers, join in the beat, whilst we all should go on, and take up positions as usual. This resolution having been unanimously carried, we sent a messenger with our 'salaam' to his highness. This is the polite Oriental way of intimating to a person that a visit from him would be agreeable to you. Accordingly, he stepped out of his tent, and appeared before us.

I never saw a stranger sight in the jungle. He was in the prime of life, of middle height, and active figure. But his costume, considering the circumstances, was truly astonishing. He was dressed in the gaudiest and richest of silks, and was loaded with large gems. How such a being was to get through a thorny jungle, or encounter any of the unforeseen accidents that so often accompany a tiger hunt, seemed to us all to be one of those things that no one can understand.

No wonder that he gladly accepted a commanding seat in the howdah! Just before the start, however, he vanished for a few seconds, and reappeared transformed into the proper colour for shooting in the jungles. This he had effected by having himself tied up in a thin brown outer covering, taking in everything, even to the diadem on his head,—much as a best piece of furniture is covered up for 'work-day' occasions. In this improved condition he took his place in the howdah, and we all sallied forth.

The nullah was beaten, but without putting up any game. One part of it was inaccessible, even to the elephants. Here the floods of ages had massed the debris of fallen trees and branches in a singular manner. The huge standing trunks had formed props for what would otherwise have been washed away by the torrent. The masses thus collected had gradually joined one another, and formed an almost impregnable stronghold of five or six acres for such animals as tigers and panthers. We decided to enter this on foot rather than give up the chance of killing the tiger. I was followed by the rajah, who kept close at my heels, and after him came about half-a-dozen of his best fighting-men, literally armed to the teeth, and looking extraordinarily fierce.

Just as we were balancing ourselves on a sort of reef of rotten vegetable matter, a great cry arose of 'Bāgh! bāgh!' Tiger! tiger! I hastened in the required direction, followed by the rajah, and soon saw a madly-excited and scantily-clothed beater, with his arms and legs rigidly extended, as though prepared for flight in any direction, and pointing with a stick at a heap of the debris I have described. I was soon at his side, and peering down the dark hole which he was indicating. I at once saw a patch of tiger skin at the bottom; but whether it were only a portion of a cub that I was looking at, or whether the whole family were hiding together, it was impossible to say. The entrance and retreat generally looked too small to admit of a full-grown animal being there, but, owing to the nature of the debris, there was no feeling certain on this head. I decided on aiming at what I could see, and firing. My shot was answered by three tiger-cubs rushing frantically out. I looked around; the rajah was still behind me, but all the natives, including his armed followers, had evidently been safe up trees at the first inspiriting cry of 'Tiger!' Calling loudly for assistance, I ran after the cub which seemed most likely to escape, and as it darted into a bush I pounced on the nape of its neck, and held it down, whilst it spat, growled, and whirled its claws about with much vigour. It was too small to be dangerous, but as it had its teeth it could certainly have done one a good deal of temporary damage. I was soon surrounded by the beaters, four of whom I caused to grasp the feet of the cub, one man to each foot. This was neatly executed, and then a fifth man spread out a large cloth that he had, and in less time than it takes to tell, the tiger became a parcel slung on a pole, and carried by a couple of men. The beaters meanwhile captured the other two cubs in their own fashion. Unfortunately one had been so badly hit by my bullet that it had to be destroyed. I kept the one I had caught myself till she was about six months old. She may possibly appear again in these pages under the name of 'Pusseytoo.' She had to be christened thus, as her sister got named first, and was called 'Pussey.' At the time of their capture we thought these cubs were not more than a week old, but I am now convinced their age was little, if at all, under two months. Their teeth were well through, and they could run a good pace through the jungle,—very different to some others that I captured some years afterwards, and which will be described in due course.

I feel but little doubt that the tigress which I shot whilst riding Roghanath Guj was the mother of these young things, as there were signs about her of having cubs. Perhaps the roaring heard by the villagers was the voice of the father coming to look after them at night; or it may even have been occasioned by the young animals themselves, as they prowled round the villages in search of such carrion and offal as they could find. Their bad condition would also favour such a supposition. This question, however, would only be interesting to lovers of natural history, and need not be further discussed here. At all events we said good-bye to the sporting rajah and the Beria ravine, to whomsoever it may have belonged, without seeing any more tigers, whether young or old.

CHAPTER VI.

THE next day we returned to the Gātie ravine, where we had lately bagged the large panther at which even the vultures had turned up their noses. It was certain that there was a fine tigress in this locality, and it was not long before she was viewed by some of the natives, many of whom had ascended trees to the height of forty or fifty feet. She appeared, however, but to vanish. A great deal of beating was gone through with no result, yet it was impossible she could have gone far without being seen by some of our numerous scouts, who from their high elevations commanded a bird's-eye view of the cover to its very borders. The fact was, that at some past time, half a mountain had slipped down into the stream below. Rocks were piled on one another, so vast and so uncompromisingly straight, that the elephants were unable to work their way amongst them, and of course it was out of the question to put the beaters in, even if they would have gone. I therefore bestrode the neck of Roghanath Guj, and proceeded to do all the climbing that could possibly be accomplished. Having got to the bottom of the ravine, I took the up-stream course, followed by the female elephant, Mānut Dār, with Peyma in the howdah. My own elephant had a cloth over its back, tied on with ropes; this formed quite a little playground for the mahout, Ghassee Ram, and the under-keeper, who, having nothing to do but look after themselves, could always swing themselves by the rigging to the sheltered side of the elephant.

I had not gone far when we were brought to a standstill by the rocks. On the right was the mountain-side, which was quite perpendicular to beyond the range of vision. On the left were several large rocks, about twenty feet high, and in front was a sort of step just the height of Roghanath Guj's back. In the centre where we were standing there was only room for the two elephants to turn. 'This,' said Peyma, pointing to the rocks on the left, 'is where the tigress ought to be. It is the centre of the position.'

In vain, however, did we peer in through all the chinks we could find; no glimpse of the tigress was to be obtained. So, after waiting some time, I said I would go back, and see if I could find some weak place among the rocks up which the elephant might be urged, and thus take the position in rear. Mānut Dār did not like being left behind, and no sooner was I out of sight than she began to complain, and that, too, in a voice fully worthy of her great frame. Probably all elephants have the same deep note; but I have only heard two make use of it, namely Bahadur Guj when waiting for his evening feed of baked cakes, and Mānut Dār when in a state of alarm. The latter far surpassed the former in vocal efforts, and on this occasion she produced a sound exactly like distant thunder, which must have vibrated under all the nearer rocks. At all events, the tigress rushed from under the very block that the elephant was standing next to, and fled up towards where the guns were posted; but she stopped short before any of the sportsmen had seen her. As it happened, I was working Roghanath Guj upwards, and in the right direction. Just as he had surmounted some large and difficult boulders, a man nearly at the top of a neighbouring tree said he could see the tigress crouching behind some large stones. I made fresh efforts to get forward on the elephant, but was soon stopped by an insurmountable barrier. I was wondering what I should do next, when I suddenly saw the tigress looking at me through a leafy screen not more than forty yards off. The elephant was standing quite still, so I aimed steadily at her chest, and fired. When the smoke cleared, nothing whatever was to be seen of her; but the man in the tree called out that she was dead. As it was simply impossible for the elephant to advance another inch, I asked him, previous to dismounting, if he were sure the beast was killed. He now said he thought it was alive, but that, at any rate, he could distinctly see it lying down, and ended by inviting me to climb with my gun up to his lofty perch, and survey the animal for myself! This was like inviting Roghanath Guj to spring up the perpendicular rocks in front of him! I decided, therefore, that I must dismount; so, letting my gun hang down my back, I slid down the elephant's tail, and made towards a small tree about half-way between me and the tigress. It was of small pole-like growth, and would admit of my getting ten feet or so up it. As I had gained about twenty feet in altitude after dismounting, I sincerely hoped I should be able to make out the enemy as soon as I should be in position, otherwise nothing would remain but to advance to the very spot where the animal was concealed. This would have been highly dangerous, as the reader may well imagine, when he considers the nature of the ground. On arriving at the foot of the little tree, I cast a scrutinizing glance at the heap of black rocks, now so much nearer, and among which the scout in the high banyan tree still proclaimed that he could see the unmoving form of the recumbent beast. So much, therefore, depended upon what the extra eight or ten feet that I could get out of this tree would do for me, that I mounted to the greatest height I could attain with my back to the foe. Then I turned round to see whether I was to be rewarded or disappointed. It was all right. There in front of me lay the tigress across a large stone; I could only see the centre of her body. I thought she must be dead, or she would never have remained in such an uncomfortable position. I raised my gun, and aimed at the middle of her back; the bullet entered near her spine. She neither moved nor uttered any sound; but still I thought, being quite alone at my post, there could be no harm in having both barrels loaded before making an advance. I therefore, with my eyes fixed on the dead animal, slowly opened my gun, took a cartridge from my pocket, and placed it in the breech. I just looked down for a second to adjust the pin of the cartridge to the nick made for it, when I suddenly heard a mighty rush, combined with a loud roar. The tigress was gone, and that too with a speed that rendered her invisible to me. By the sound of her voice, and the crashing of the dense corinda bushes, which, tough and terribly armed as they were with long thorns, yielded to her like reeds before the wind, I could hear that she had flown down the declivity, and again taken up her position under the rock whence she had been started by the powerful tones of Mānut Dār.

In less than ten minutes I had again brought Roghanath Guj to the point already described. I stepped from his head on to the rock that ran across the bed of the gorge, when I was signalled to by my friends on the heights above, who were making the best of their way down the long, steep, and difficult declivity to join me. We were soon five in number. A few feet from us was the mouth of the cave. To this, supported by some spare gun-bearers, we advanced. We could see the tigress crouching at the bottom of the lair. At a given signal we fired a volley; and I could just make out the dim outline of the beast as she charged almost into our faces. Owing, doubtless, to the dense volume of smoke, she missed her aim, as no one was seized. For a few seconds nothing could be seen, and we naturally supposed she was lying dead at our feet. Far from this, however; when the atmosphere cleared, she was not even in sight. As the elephant was standing conveniently below me in charge of the mahout, Ghassee Ram, I scrambled on to his broad back, and told the keeper to drive round the corner of the nearest boulder. This he proceeded to do slowly, and craning his neck forward to the utmost of his power, suddenly he stopped, leant back, and said, 'I see the beast.' I ordered him to drive on; but he refused, saying, 'She is standing up, and about to spring.' I therefore changed places with him, and at once came face to face with the tigress. Poor beast! I shall never forget her aspect. She was standing up, and trying to look at us, but her eyes were rolling so fearfully that I doubt if she could have made out anything distinctly. This was, I thought, a symptom of impending death; but it gave the animal such a ghastly appearance that I do not wonder at an impressionable Indian being awed by it. I lost no time in putting a bullet through her heart, and she fell dead at last. I then dismounted, and went to examine the spot where I had first fired at her from the head of the elephant. Here, at the base of the stone across which she was lying when I fired from the little tree, was a large pool of blood. As the animal had been directly facing me when I fired my first shot, the bullet must have entered her chest, and she would probably have died where she was had she been let alone. Perhaps my second bullet may have opened a passage for some coagulated blood, and thus actually have afforded her some temporary relief. This may seem improbable; but it is only on some supposition of this sort that the facts, for the strict truth of which I can vouch, can be accounted for.

At our next camping-ground we were attacked by enemies considered by many far more formidable than the tigers themselves. I refer to bees. These insects suspend their shield-shaped combs, often a yard or more in diameter, from the boughs of the great forest trees, or from the projecting point of some giant cliff. They are generally in practically inaccessible positions; but even when easy to reach, no one seems to interfere with this particular species. I believe the natives have some superstitious regard for them. At any rate they will always take the honey of the smaller kind when opportunity offers. I did not care for the produce of these little fellows, as it was too sweet and mawkish. I could never induce the aborigines to bring me any of the other sort, which would probably have resembled our English honey, as the bees themselves were in size and character much the same as those belonging to the hives in European lands. If so, it would be a great addition to jungle fare in the hot weather, when there is very little of a toothsome nature to regale oneself upon. On the present occasion there were perhaps half-a-dozen combs amongst the highest boughs of our camp trees, and their inhabitants were showing signs of unusual activity. What had put them out, it was not easy to say; perhaps our cooking fires, as they detest the smell of smoke. Suddenly they began to pitch down, like large drops of rain, and fix on to some man or animal with great precision, inflicting a painful sting. Fortunately, one always has such a large following in the East, that in a few minutes, and consequently before the attack had become general, all the animals, and even some of the tents, had been removed beyond the territory which these little tyrants considered their own. Then all was peace, except when one particular butler showed himself. They seemed to recognize him at once, and immediately set upon him. I believe there are many instances on record of bees distinguishing particular people. We were fortunate in getting off so easily. Sometimes serious mischief ensues from one of their onslaughts. I once knew an officer who for the time was blinded by them, and in his efforts to escape, fell over a precipice, and broke some of his bones!

The next village we halted at was called Ruttongurh. It was the stronghold of no less a personage than Peyma, and the birthplace of himself and sons. It may be supposed, therefore, that we were received with really affectionate cordiality by the inhabitants. It was a large village, containing perhaps a thousand souls, but boasting of no products beyond the necessaries of life. The elephants were stationed just outside the walls, and our tents were erected under a fine grove of trees immediately below them. Our rest during the first night of our stay here was sadly broken in upon by the breaking loose of two vicious ponies. How great is often the power of the meanest creatures for evil! The night was dark; the syces (or grooms) were lazy; no one seemed able or willing to capture these little wretches. At intervals of, say, half-an-hour, just as one was getting off to sleep again, they would tear through the camp at racing speed, screaming as though pursued by demons. At the first sound of their approach from the jungle, where they might just as well have stayed, every village dog made ready to join the senseless 'kick up.' Even the elephants at last thought something must be wrong, and began to trumpet. Now it was anything but pleasant to think of these huge animals running wildly about in a state of panic. Roghanath Guj, had he happened to take the line of our little shikar tents, would have carried them all away at the end of his tusks without knowing they were there, whilst his great feet would have come down on our beds and reduced them to splinters, with us in them! Neither of the ponies belonged to me, so I ardently hoped they would both break their necks among the tent ropes, or that, as they flew into the jungle, one at least would be pounced upon by the large tiger we had come to shoot. Anything was better than getting up, as that would have banished sleep for certain during the rest of the night. Nothing, however, happened to these little miscreants till dawn of day, when they were caught by their careless attendants, tied up, fed, and petted, just as though they had spent the night in meritorious efforts to promote our well-being.

The next day we were prevented going after the tiger by the occurrence of a tremendous thunderstorm. I have never witnessed a greater deluge of rain. It was accompanied by such a high wind, that in a few minutes one tent alone was left standing. Into this we all crowded, and passed a portion of our lives perched on tables, beds, and such other pieces of camp furniture as appeared above high-water mark. Land was nowhere visible. Everything seemed to grow out of water. Rain, however, in the early part of May never lasts long. In two hours' time it was quite fine again, and delightfully cool. By the evening, nothing was to be seen of the flood except pretty, cool-looking ponds wherever there were depressions in the soil. I could not help enjoying the change of climate, although no doubt it was very bad for our sport. Now the tigers would find water all over the country, and besides this, owing to the freshness of the air and the coolness of the earth, they would set off at the first alarm, and travel at a rapid pace to great distances. Happily, our gloomy forebodings are not always realized, for during the night after the thunderstorm the tiger was reported to have killed a fine cow within a mile of our tents. He had been hunted before, and was a well-known animal. Each succeeding escape had made him more and more cunning. He had learnt before moving to study all the trees and points of vantage from which experience had told him he might expect the fire of his enemies.

The shikarries therefore decided to ring him with a very wide circle of scouts on trees and hill-tops, and then to guide us on foot up to the kill, in the hopes that he would not move till we should confront him. All being ready, we proceeded to execute this plan, which was not so easy as it seemed, for we had to thread our way up a dry, shallow watercourse, full of thorny bushes and stones of all sizes, amongst which it was impossible to move without making much more noise than was desirable.

We had not proceeded more than two hundred yards up this watercourse before we perceived a golden-coloured body lying on the ground among the underwood. For a moment I thought it might be the tiger, but it was only the dead cow, the inside of which had alone been eaten so far. Simultaneously with our arrival at the 'kill,' a distant scout shouted out that the tiger was in retreat. Peyma instantly turned to the left, and made us all run as hard as we could to a point whence we could be thrown out in a line across a tract which he thought the animal would be sure to cross. We had no time to hesitate about our positions. Each took the post assigned him at once, and made the best of it. The tiger did not keep us waiting long. I saw him break close to one of my friends who was standing in the fork of a tree. He fired, and hit the animal behind the shoulder. The beast at once charged, and I felt intensely anxious for my friend's safety, as he was within reach of this very large and enraged brute. Owing, I believe, to the sportsman's clothes matching remarkably well with the colour of the timber he was on, the tiger had not clearly made him out, and so charged headlong past him, presenting a very fine appearance as he galloped over a bald knoll, lashing his tail, and looking vindictively up at the high rocks, where he could discern numbers of his enemies, but all out of reach.

He was soon out of sight, and we all assembled to decide upon how he was to be followed up. It was known that he was badly hit, and that he would consequently not be likely to travel far. He had disappeared into a tract of dense thorn-bush mixed with high tussocks of jungle grass. Peyma led us round this, and placed us in such trees as could be found; they were small, few, and far between. Peyma was to lead the beat in the howdah borne by Mānut Dār. As I had been told off to occupy a tree, I had told Ghassee Ram on no account to bring Roghanath Guj into the jungle without me. How he disobeyed, and with what result, will be seen further on.

I had not been more than a few minutes in my tree when I heard the tiger cautiously prowling round it, but could not see him; every moment I expected him to emerge close to me. I made no sound whatever, but I suppose he winded me. Suddenly the stealthy noises died away, and were quickly succeeded by a loud uproar as of direst confusion. Rifles were cracking, men shouting, elephants trumpeting, and above all the tiger roared with unusual grandeur. In the absence of my elephant I sprang to the ground, and, followed by my gun-bearer 'Chowpatty,' I hastened to the scene of action. In the centre of the position I came upon one of my friends who had assisted at this second denouement. As all was for the moment quiet, I climbed up beside him to obtain whatever information he could give me. The tiger, it seems, had come towards him, and he had not failed to wound it again. Then the leader of our party with another friend had got into the howdah with Peyma, and began to look for the wounded animal. Of course, no one who knows the native Indian character will be surprised to hear that Ghassee Ram took one of Peyma's sons on Roghanath Guj, who had nothing but a wadded cloth on his back to keep off the sun, and commenced to meander about this dense cover just as if they were looking for a stray sheep! Ghassee Ram had not even thought it worth while to bestride the elephant's neck, but just reclined, like his companion, whose name was Goolba, on the comfortable broad back of his great steed. Their conversation probably ran thus:—

GHASSEE RAM.—'Oh, brother! what do you think will be the price of flour at the next village after leaving Ruttongurh.'

GOOLBA.—'Well, for the next march or two the price is always the same; but who can tell what it will be beyond that!'

GHASSEE RAM.—'Certainly in this world everything depends on "Nusseeb" (Fate).'

Such was their position when the wounded tiger sprang from his ambush with a short, fierce cry, and fixed on to the flank of the elephant, who, to get rid of his antagonist, rolled on to that side. Ghassee Ram and Goolba, being totally unprepared for any emergencies, had tumbled off in the opposite direction. The tiger, finding it could not make much impression on Roghanath Guj, fortunately made off, without observing the two men on the ground; and the elephant, finding itself riderless, had marched himself back to the village. According to some accounts, Ghassee Ram was in a dying state, if not dead. Goolba, whom I encountered walking about, not frightened, only much excited, said he did not know whether Ghassee Ram had been injured by the tiger or not, but that he did not think he could be in a dying state, as he had seen him disappearing with a stick in the direction of our camp. So much, for the present, was all that was known of Roghanath Guj. As to Mānut Dār, the tiger leaving the first elephant had rushed at her, and caught her by the hind leg. This so terrified and demoralized her, that she set off as fast as she could, not for our present quarters, but for a village we had previously occupied, some five or six miles distant. Two of our party were in the howdah, and a dreadful time they had of it. Nothing could stop her. She skirted the edges of precipices with rotten mud sides, and ran foul of many trees. The howdah became displaced, and the contents were all shaken out at intervals as she pursued her wild career. Thus both the elephants were gone, but as far as we two knew either might be brought back at any moment; so we decided to wait for some time. At a distance of about two hundred yards we could see one of our native followers perched as high as he could get on another stump of a tree (there were no large ones about here), not looking altogether comfortable. Suddenly this man dropped to the ground and ran breathless up to us.

'Sahib,' he said, 'the tiger is lying growling under that tree. I could bear it no longer by myself, and have risked being killed to get to you.'

On this I got down, mounted my Galloway 'Krishna,' and rode right round the tree at a distance of twenty or thirty yards. I could neither see nor hear the tiger. I then took up my position, still on horseback, immediately under the tree, and called out to the man to come up to me, accompanied by my horse-keeper. Of course if the tiger had started, it would have been after me. Krishna being of a wild and fiery nature would probably have broken my neck, which would have given ample time to the two black men to get back to their refuge. I should, of course, have endeavoured to lead the tiger past my friend, who would have shot it; but with such an irrational being as Krishna to manage, it is doubtful if I could have done this. The two men, as it turned out, reached me without the tiger showing himself, so I sent away the man and horse, and then mounted the forked stump, accompanied by its former occupant.

'There,' he exclaimed at once, pointing with agitation to a dark bush about thirty yards off, 'there is the tiger! It is lying with its head between its paws looking at us.'

'That,' I said, 'my good man, I can assure you is nothing but a black stone with some long dead yellow grass standing about it.'

'No, no,' he said, 'it is the tiger; I am certain of it. Have I not watched it for an hour?'

All this I shouted back to my friend, who said I had better fire at the object, and then, if it did not move, we would go together and inspect it. We did all this, and found it just as I had said. It was now close on sunset, and too late to make any fresh start, although we were joined, if I remember, at this moment by our two friends out of Mānut Dār's howdah.

I galloped to our camp as fast as I could to see what had really happened to Ghassee Ram. There he was, laid out on a charpoy (bedstead) under the shadow of Roghanath Guj. Notwithstanding the intense heat of the weather, he was buried, head and all, under a perfect pile of dirty clothing, some belonging to himself, and some to the elephant. Around this funereal couch squatted a dozen or two sympathizers of both sexes. 'Dear me,' I said, 'what is the matter? Ghassee Ram, speak to me!' Thus exhorted, Ghassee Ram displayed a pale countenance, with eyes larger than their wont, and shining with a glassy stare. I said, 'What is the matter? Did the tiger get hold of you?'

'Certainly,' he answered. 'What else could have happened?'

'Show me,' I said. Hereupon the assistants raised one of his arms, swathed in cloths till it was the size of an ordinary person's body. The patient groaned so dismally that I said I would not look at it, for we had a doctor with us who must be in before long. I turned to go, but before I had gone six steps I said to myself, Suppose he should be slowly bleeding to death? He looks as though he were, and his voice is so faint. I returned, and ordered the wounded limb to be exposed to view. The chief nurses slowly unwound the successive bandages, whilst the poor mahout uttered plaintive sounds from time to time. As the last fold was removed I was really staring with a highly-wrought gaze. Nothing, absolutely nothing! Speechless, I looked around for an explanation. All maintained the same awe-struck expression, including the patient. You see they had made up their minds to be horrified. At last a solemn voice said, 'Doosera hai,' which means, 'It is the other arm,' and the same performance was gone through with that limb, but, of course, without any anxiety on my part. The second arm had had some skin grazed off by falling on the hard ground, and one ankle was certainly sprained from the same cause, but not very badly. This was all that had really happened to Ghassee Ram, but his nerves were so shaken, that I seriously asked the doctor, as soon as he arrived, whether he might not die of fright. He said the man might do so, but that it was not likely.

I now learnt that Mānut Dār really had run all the way back to our former encampment. The mahout, it seems, had worked with extraordinary, but perhaps mistaken energy, to stop her. For this purpose he had incessantly plied the goad till the top of her poor head was like a ploughed field. Nothing, however, had the desired effect, till she reached the village for which she was making, and rushed, all dishevelled, into a ruined court-yard, which she evidently considered a safe refuge. Her much-tried passengers alighted and proceeded to take a view of the terrified animal and the wrecked howdah. In the course of the inspection the mahout passed in front of her with the much-used goad in his hand. This instrument she whipped from him with her trunk, and deftly threw it over the wall. This was, I thought, a very pretty way of expressing firm yet gentle reproof for the wrongs the man had inflicted on her.

The howdah having been righted, and the elephant calmed a little, she brought the party back to the camp at Ruttongurh. When we were all together again, a consultation was held, and it was decided that we would all go back to the jungle the first thing in the morning, take up fresh positions, and that I should ride Roghanath Guj in quest of the missing tiger.

How we carried out this plan, and with what result, will be duly set forth in the next chapter.

CHAPTER VII.

THE next morning by six o'clock we were ready to start again for the spot where we had last seen the tiger. It was not more than three miles distant. But an elephant does not care to travel over three miles an hour, so it was past seven by the time we arrived, and the sun was consequently getting hot. Roghanath Guj at once recognized the *locale*, and showed a strong desire to renew the combat of the day before, in which, though not considered to have been hurt, he had received a smack from his antagonist which had left the print of the tiger's foot and claws on his left side.

Selecting the tree which I had occupied the evening before, as a centre, I began to search the jungle by going round it in ever-widening circles. At the first high and dark screen of bushes that I came to, Roghanath hesitated for an instant, but I had only to speak firmly to him, and press his neck with my knees, and he at once understood that we were to be prepared for any encounter. From this moment, coming to anything he could not see through, he would plunge in and come out again with his head erect and ears raised. On one occasion, as we neared a very thick bush, he showed signs of great excitement. He rushed upon and trampled it, uttering low sounds of rage at the same time. The tiger had lain for a long time in this bush, and had left a large dark pool of blood in the centre of it. This stain, combined with the strong smell, had been mistaken by the elephant for the tiger itself; and I was glad to see that old Guj was evidently determined not to be taken unawares this time. He was not, however, destined to put forth his valour on this occasion, for shortly afterwards the under-keeper, who was sitting behind on the elephant's back, espied the tiger lying stretched dead on a piece of open ground at no great distance from us. I took the elephant up to within twenty yards of the beast, but so great is the sagacity of these animals, that he was well aware it was no longer living, and refused to take the slightest notice of it. The tiger proved to be a splendid animal, but I forgot to take a note of its measurements. It was now about eight o'clock in the morning, and we were only just in time to save the skin, for decomposition had already set in. Yet, notwithstanding this circumstance, and the fact that it had disgorged its last meal, not a single vulture, or other carrion bird, had ventured even to hover over the dead monarch. We had thought that the presence of these birds would be certain to indicate the whereabouts of the dead beast, especially if he should have died in the open, as he did. But such was not the case. As long as such beasts as tigers and bears have their skins on them, though they may be quite dead, all the inferior animals seem still to fear them.

I cannot better conclude the story of this adventure than by saying a few words in defence of poor Ghassee Ram. Should the reader persevere with the perusal of these pages, he will see that this mahout could behave with much coolness and courage under very trying circumstances, and I think we may account for his panic on the present occasion by pointing out that hitherto he had always relied blindly on fate, and had invariably escaped all serious accidents. Surely he would think that to begin now to act for himself would be to provoke this benign influence into deserting him, to say nothing of the trouble that reflecting for himself would entail. No; fate had always managed very well so far, and no doubt if not interfered with would continue ever favourable. That so good and pious a Hindoo should without an instant's warning suddenly see the head of an immense tiger protruding from the back of his own elephant, within a few inches of his person, open-mouthed, fiery-eyed, and roaring fiercely, was bad enough; but furthermore, to be pitched off that back on which he had sat for so many years in perfect confidence, and left alone with Goolba, helplessly prone upon the ground, was worse, and calculated to shake the faith of a lifetime. In less than a week from the day of his misfortune he was on his legs again. His ankle and his self-possession were both fully restored. He still professed the same devout faith in destiny, but with this difference, that henceforth he was more prepared for its vagaries. 'For,' he said to me one day when talking this matter over, 'how can a poor man like me tell *what* may be written in his fate?'

From Ruttongurh we went to a ravine called 'Kokee.' It was a magnificent rift. The rocks, or rather cliffs, the trees, and the water, were all on an unusual scale of size and splendour. From where we entered, to the upper end, it may have been a couple of miles in length, and varied at the bottom from one to four hundred yards in width. In places it would run out into rough-looking amphitheatres, full of rocks, trees, and deep, clear pools of water, surrounded by overhanging bushes. We were soon placed in a line across this ravine, but we were not all able to secure safe posts for the first shot, as the trees and rocks fell short at one or two of the places that had to be guarded.

The perfect silence was soon broken by the sudden clang of the 'beat.' All the birds and animals were rudely roused from their mid-day siesta. The Lungoor or Entellus monkeys were very numerous here. They have a loud and very deep note, which would be no disgrace to a tiger, and would always be supposed by the novice to proceed from that animal, were he not previously cautioned against such a mistake. During this beat they gradually formed a large troop in front of the beaters, always, when possible, keeping high up among the trees, though they would occasionally have to descend to cross an open space. As they came nearer, in addition to being heard, they could be seen grasping the more pliant boughs, and shaking them violently with rage, but whether at the beaters or a tiger it was impossible to say. In the midst of this clamour the report of a gun was heard from the post occupied by the leader of our party. In such a jungle as there was in the Kokee rift a tiger would almost always contrive to disappear, however well shot, and this one was no exception to the rule. For a long time we could not find him, though we were sure he could not have gone far. At last a sharp-eyed native discovered a patch of black and yellow stripes in a deep pool of water, and underneath a thick overhanging bush. It was soon pulled out, and found to have been shot close to the heart, perhaps through it. Strange to say, a fish, about five inches long, had pushed its head into the hole made by the bullet, and had been unable to withdraw it, so it had died with its head so firmly fixed in 'chancery' that there was some difficulty in extricating it.

After disposing of the tiger we were taken to the head of the ravine to beat for bears. Here we went through many caves which had a quantity of large bees' nests hanging from their roofs; many of them were within easy reach, but, of course, we had no time to try and take any honey. Indeed, we were very glad to keep on friendly terms with these really dangerous insects. No bears, or other large game, rewarded our further efforts in the 'Kokee,' so we struck our tents and made for a place called Limrie.

Here a tigress was wounded by one of the party, but she was not put *hors de combat*, and retreated rapidly over such large rocks and narrow pathways that the elephants could not be made any use of. We therefore followed her on foot. She was bleeding a good deal, which made it easy to make out the track. Peyma said she was heading for a very extensive piece of strong jungle two or three miles distant, and that if we did not come up with her before she got there, we should have to abandon the chase till the next day. We therefore got on as fast as we could, and at one time we thought success was to crown our undertaking, as we came to a cave where she had evidently lain a considerable time, for there was a large patch of blood in the centre of it. She had, however, heard our approach, and continued her flight without giving us a glimpse of her. The guiding marks now became fainter and fainter, till at last they failed us altogether. But as we had made them out nearly up to the jungle spoken of by Peyma, we felt a good deal of confidence in our plans for the future. Accordingly, the next day we entered the jungle by a detour, so as not to disturb the animal prematurely, and in the very first beat the tigress was shot by the leader of our party, and I believe she died almost without a struggle. Her wound of the day before proved very far back—indeed, close to the tail, so of course we never had had any chance of coming up with her when we were tracking her the day before, but this we could not know at the time.

My leave of absence was now drawing towards its close, and I thought it was time, with such a tedious and difficult journey before me, to turn my steps homewards. Of course, after all I had suffered at the hands of the specious Ardasseer, his very name was intolerable to me. Never as long as I live could I again face a bullock 'dawk.' I determined, therefore, to throw myself on the mercy of my friends, European and native, and thus secure a better mode of transit. The objection to posting your own relays is that you have to wait whilst the different animals or vehicles are being got to the required points.

I was now fifty or sixty miles north of Neemuch, if I remember rightly. At all events, I recollect riding one camel forty miles on the journey to that place. Here I had, of course, to halt to get my three horses out on to the road from Neemuch to Mhow, a distance of one hundred and sixty miles. Two native states, Jowra and Rutlam, lay at short distances apart, at about the middle of the total distance to be traversed. This was fortunate, as the native rulers were always very civil, and would help officers travelling through their country either with saddle horses or carriages over thirty or forty miles of the route, and then at twenty-eight miles from Mhow, up to which point there was a good metal road, the inevitable Ardasseer would have a comfortable carriage and pair of horses waiting for you. All this, together with three riding camels kindly lent, on payment, by the commissariat department, to do the first sixty miles on from Neemuch, constituted quite the best form of travelling known in those parts until recent times. Since then a railway company has appeared upon the scene, and as far as travelling is concerned, has converted that part of the country into another and a better world. Still, I think a short account of my return journey may interest my readers. Some may like to read of bygone times, others may yet have to travel a similar journey though in a different locality.

I left Neemuch at four o'clock in the afternoon on one of the sandni (riding) camels. I sat on the back seat, and allowed the native to drive me. On short trips I always drove myself, but when going long stages I found it less fatiguing to resign myself to the camel man's guidance, and occupy myself with my own thoughts. I anticipated nothing more than a pleasant, if rather a long ride, as the road was considered good and the moon would shine till midnight; and until that hour all did go very nicely.

Alas! simultaneously with the setting of the moon, we seemed to have come to the end of the made road. Perhaps we lost it in the pitch darkness which now ensued. At all events my state was sadly changed for the worse. Instead of a nice smooth gliding run of six miles an hour, we were reduced to a dreadful creep, which at all events seemed like only one mile an hour. Each step of the camel was calculated to clear a wheel-barrow. This imparted a motion to those on his back which no one could be expected to describe. I had long been unable, even with the aid of the moon, to see the fine gold hands of my watch. I was therefore denied the solace of calculating the outside distance to the next relay. This was the third and last camel, and would be succeeded at Jowra by a carriage and pair. I began to feel quite exhausted, as nothing is so trying as to feel that the animal your are on is failing. The native driver was spared this feeling. He did not care how much the animal suffered, or whether we were a few hours more or less on its back. When we found we had followed the top of a high bank instead of the proper track, till the camel stood trembling and moaning with terror on the verge of a precipice, he only said, 'Camels can't see at all well in the dark; none of them could do any better than this one under the same circumstances.'

'But,' I said, 'what are we to do now; the beast cannot go on, and there is no room to turn round?'

'Well,' he said, 'I think it could manage to sit down; then we could get off, and see exactly where to lead it to.'

This we did, and got the animal safely back into the road. I should have left the camel at this point, and walked into Jowra, but it was carrying my horse's saddle, which I did not like to lose sight of. The longest and worst journeys come to an end at last, and we arrived at the travellers' bungalow at Jowra exactly at four in the morning—thus averaging exactly five miles an hour over the total distance of sixty miles.

The journey after this was easy, and I arrived at Mhow all the better for my two months' trip, notwithstanding the great heat to which I had been exposed. The jungles which we had explored were among the hottest in the world, but the rain we met with, though so bad for sport, rendered the air cooler that year than it was on a subsequent expedition through the same country two years later. I then carried with me a trustworthy thermometer, which used to stand at ninety-seven degrees Fahrenheit when we went to bed in the open air at nine o'clock at night.

Ten days after I reached home, my servants and baggage joined me. Only those who have witnessed such an arrival can form an idea of what the procession looks like. The men look as if they would remain pillars of dust all the rest of their lives. Their clothes, with their shoes down at heel, seem only fit to be burned. The luggage generally has a most forlorn aspect, and the tents, owing to the thorny paths they have had to traverse, look like stacks of rags on the backs of the camels, who alone look according to their wont. Always rough and ungainly in appearance, and ever emitting loud, gurgling sounds of complaint, these animals never strike the observer as being happy. As a string of eight of these beasts entered my compound, loaded as I have described, and secured by the nose of one being tied to the tail of the preceding one, I called out to my travel-stained butler, who was proudly leading the way on a tiny, jaded pony, 'Is all well, and is the tiger-cub safe?'

He answered that everything was right, and pointing to a

large sort of basket or crate, he said, 'Pusseytoo is in that; and, oh, the trouble I have had with her! Nothing but my deep and well-known devotion to the sahib would have induced me to go through with the task. But I have guarded her as though she were my own life. On leaving Neemuch with new camels, I packed her, as you see, in that crate, half-filled with wet leaves, to keep her cool. It was so comfortable, she went to sleep in it at once. No sooner, however, did the camel start, than she uttered a loud roar, and tried to get out of the crate. On this the camel, thinking it had a shaitān (fiend) on its back, tore itself loose, kicked everything off its back, and fled into the jungle. Of course, my first thought, knowing your honour's mind, was for Pusseytoo. She was now quite quiet, with the crate broken, and several boxes on the top of her. I thought she was killed, and my own liver felt scorched with fright. We all rushed to the rescue, and soon restored the poor thing to consciousness. The runaway animal was soon recaptured, and Pusseytoo was transferred to the back of an aged beast, who was unable to bolt.' The poor man then further related, how that on one long march they could find no water to wet the crate with, so that Pusseytoo fainted with heat. And much more he told me to the same effect, but still I would not present him with any pecuniary reward, for fear he should thus become confirmed in his habits of exaggeration; so he had to be satisfied with grossly overcharging me for the goat's flesh which the animal had consumed on the journey.

No doubt our heroine was very glad to be let out into a nice bungalow, with lots of furniture to play about amongst, —quite like a jungle. She had a large half-bred mastiff puppy for a companion, and they were great friends. In their gambols the tigress, which had grown a great deal (especially about the paws), used to lose her temper sometimes. Then she would growl with astonishing power in one so young, sit rocking herself, with her ears laid back, and look most ferocious. The puppy, 'Whackford,' however, seemed quite unconscious of the dangerous nature of these squalls, which would probably have ended badly had I not interfered, which I always did by rushing at her with a thick stick, and shouting at her at the same time, so as to make her know and respect my voice. One of her favourite tricks was to get into my bath-tub, and with her eyes just above the brim, wait for one of the dogs to pass. Then, with a wild flourish, she would spring out, and land on the back of the astonished dog amidst a shower of spray. Whackford used to take this quite in good part, but the others were often much frightened. On one occasion, she sprang on to a greyhound called 'Pet,' who was sleeping on a sofa, and caused such a shock to his nervous system that he was, although a dog of high courage, a long time getting over it.

I have only kept two tiger-cubs; the one now under discussion, which was a female, and another that was a male. These two animals were strikingly different in their habits, and I am inclined to think, from what I have heard, that this difference in the conduct of the sexes when young, is usual in the species.

I always allowed them a great deal of liberty, and the female availed herself of it by incessantly stalking something or other. Whackford was her favourite butt, and she would manœuvre with wonderful skill to spring upon him unawares when he was lying gnawing a bone in the middle of the compound, without any grass, or stones whatever, anywhere near him. Sometimes she would lay herself out to catch one of our legs in a fond embrace as we were proceeding unconsciously, intent upon our business or pleasure.

One morning I was standing outside my front door, when I saw Mr. Chunder Mull, a native banker, with whom I had some dealings, alight from his lank and miserable grey pony, at my garden gate, and begin making the best of his way towards me. Chunder Mull, physically, was even more decrepit than his steed. Neither of them ever stirred from home except in the interests of business. Then much furniture, surmounted by a mattress and pillows, was fixed upon the half-starved brute, so that Chunder Mull might recline at ease, and think over what he would say on arriving at his destination.

The banker presented an extraordinary appearance as he made his way up the gravelled drive. He was elderly, tall, and may have been intended by nature for a fine man. But many years of sitting cross-legged in front of his money-boxes, with his ledgers before him, had quite unfitted him for any other phases of life. His person generally had become much distended, whilst his long legs had got very thin and uncertain in their movements, so that he would pursue an erratic course, from one side of the path to the other. Add to this, that his upper man was fantastically draped in flowing garments, whilst the legs, from being so seldom seen, had nothing on them at all, and you will have some idea of what Chunder Mull looked like as he made his way towards me on that memorable morning. I was not pleased to see this person, but one should always receive a money-lender courteously. I therefore called out in cheerful tones, 'Ah, friend Chunder Mull, how are you? What can I do for you this morning?' and so forth.

At this the advancing banker looked up, then suddenly became as one rooted to the ground. His eyes were fixed on a tuft of grass a few yards from him, with a glassy stare. I followed the direction of his gaze, and saw just the eyes of Pusseytoo gleaming over this long grass with indescribable ferocity at his nearest withered leg! I at once cried out that the cub only meant play, and would not hurt him.

The sound of my voice broke the spell under which he was labouring. He turned, and, without uttering a sound, seemed literally to fly from the premises, for his flowing turban and muslin shawls fluttered like wings in the morning breeze. In less time than it takes to relate, he was in the centre of his pile of bedding, and by some occult means had actually induced the poor old pony to venture on a gallop. Thus they vanished, like a strange vision, amidst the laughter of those who were looking on. I never saw this man again, as nothing would induce him to venture near my quarters any more; so, of course, I felt bound to pay him all that he asked for keeping my establishment going in my absence, without taxing his bill; thus, I think, proving the proposition on politeness that I started with.

The conduct of my pet, however, soon became such as to convince me that tigers should either be shot or kept behind strong bars. One day an unusually loud commotion was heard in the direction of the servants' quarters. Pusseytoo, it seems, had pounced upon a duck in real earnest, and had devoured it in spite of the opposition of my followers. Still, being fond of the animal, I was weakly indulgent, and still allowed her to roam at large about the grounds, till one day, when I was standing outside the stables, she suddenly flew past me like a flash of lightning, and flung herself on to the neck of a very large and valuable milch-goat. The goat uttered loud and dismal cries, which would soon have ended in suffocation, as the cub's fangs were buried in her throat. I sprang forward and grasped the aggressor by the nape of the neck. On this she just freed one paw from the goat, and aimed a blow at me which opened the sleeve of my coat from the shoulder to the wrist. I now picked up a tent-peg, which was lying close to hand, and gave her what I thought would be a sufficient tap on the head to induce her to drop the unfortunate victim; but this only made her tighten her clutch, so I was obliged to go on tapping harder and harder, till at last she dropped off partially stunned. After this I kept her on the chain; and any one who was disengaged used to take her for walks.

She was once invited to enliven a children's garden party; so I ordered a shut-up bullock carriage for the occasion. She seemed to approve of the vehicle till it began to move, when she made a sudden bound at the front window, and nearly caught the driver by the back. I met this by dragging her on to the floor, and holding her down exactly as I had done when I had caught her in the jungle, but, of course, her greatly increased size made the operation much more difficult on this occasion. All this time the little animal was making a great noise, and I was naturally anxious to get out of this cart. I was so placed that looking out of the window was a matter of difficulty. At last, however, wondering at our non-arrival, I contrived to take a look round, and was dismayed to find that the driver had forgotten where we were to go to, and we were now much farther off the scene of the festivities than we had been at starting.

I roared to the wretched man to stop, which he did ; but he would not open the door. However, two other natives, who were passing, when they understood that the tiger was chained, turned the handle, and ran away. Pusseytoo and I then projected ourselves violently into the ditch at the side of the road, and she took refuge in the neighbouring hedge, where she immediately became calm and placid. I then led her home, changed my clothes, which had got into a dreadful state, and proceeded, leading her on foot, to the entertainment, where she behaved so well that the children were all exhorted by their parents and guardians to try and grow up like her! The end of this exemplary creature was, however, sad.

I gave her to a friend who was sending a male cub home to England, and was anxious to get a young tigress, so as to make a pair. Ever since the unfortunate episode of the goat, poor Pusseytoo had been subject to occasional fits, and she died of one the very day she was to have started on her journey to Europe.

The next and last tiger cub that I reared was a male. I captured it, together with its two little brothers, after shooting the mother, who sprang from the very den in which two years previously I and my friends had shot another tigress, as I have already described. These little animals were not a quarter the size of those first captured; yet as they had their eyes open, and were quite awake as to what was going on, they must have been at least ten days old. Their gums were quite smooth, the teeth not having yet pierced the skin. All three were in very good condition, and very beautiful to behold. When I entered the den they all huddled together in the farthest corner, and winked and blinked at me in a most comical manner. I had two friends with me, so we each took one as a nursling.

The behaviour of these cubs as they grew up was very different to that of Pusseytoo. They were all much better tempered; and I never saw mine attempt to stalk anything. He prowled about in a calm and dignified manner, taking life quite seriously; and this, I believe, was the case with his two brothers. One of them I saw when it had grown to a dangerous size. He was very gentle, and quite healthy; but I think he died before he was one year old.

Mine I presented to the head of a mercantile house in Bombay, by whom, I believe, it was sent to Vienna as a present to the Zoological Gardens of that city. As this animal had always enjoyed perfect health till the moment it left me, there is every reason to hope, not only that it reached its destination in safety, but that it may even now be living there in a good state of preservation. If alive, it would in this year of 1883 be about seven years old. I do not know to what age tigers may attain in a state of captivity, though this is a point which must be well known to keepers of menageries and others who may be interested in the question. As to the age they may be expected to reach roaming at large in their native jungles, it is hard to see how to determine on satisfactory data; but their lives, when free, must be much longer than when imprisoned. In a state of nature these animals take an immense deal of exercise during the night, and also obtain a much greater change of food than many persons would suppose. Not only do they prey on a great variety of animals, ranging from porcupines to buffaloes, but they always begin by devouring the stomach of their victims, by which they obtain a very large amount of vegetable diet. Of course it is from the want of suitable food and sufficient exercise that so many of these creatures when in confinement show an arched back that, at all events, looks like curvature of the spine. This, being a form in which they are never seen when wild, must represent impaired strength and a shortened life.

CHAPTER VIII.

THE TERAI.

I WAS still at Mhow, when for my next annual holiday I was fortunate enough to obtain an invitation from a very good sportsman to shoot with him in the Terai. I could only get leave of absence for two months, and, but for the railway, I could never have attempted to go so far. I started on the 1st of April, taking with me six or seven servants, and everything else that I was likely to require, such as oilman's stores, wine, tents, etc.

I was very comfortable on the journey. Owing to the heat, there is not much passenger traffic at that time of the year; I was consequently able to have a large first-class carriage to myself, which on this line struck me as peculiarly lofty and roomy. They were also furnished with a cooling apparatus, which worked very well. It consisted of screens of kuskus fibre, through which water was kept dripping regularly from a reservoir above. The kuskus, when wet, exhales a delightful fragrance, so that the air, as it rushed through these screens, was not only beautifully cooled, but also sweetly scented. The difference between the inside of my temporary abode and the outer air, can only be guessed at by those who have never travelled under the same circumstances. The horse-boxes, for instance, of which there were several attached to my train, would have afforded a striking contrast. So great was the heat, that the litter on which the animals were standing took fire! This occasioned a great outcry, but the fire had luckily been discovered by the men in charge in time to get it extinguished without any loss of life. Had I gone direct from Mhow to Moradabad, I should have been about two nights and three days in the train; but as I was passing within a short distance of Agra, I determined to visit that interesting city. I should only have to break the journey by one day, and I thought then I should never have another opportunity of visiting the famous Taj, and the splendid palatial ruins for which this place is so justly celebrated.

It was past seven o'clock in the evening when I reached the hotel, and quite dark. There was to be no moon that night, which was very unfortunate, as one is not considered to have seen the Taj properly without viewing it, once at least, in a flood of Oriental moonlight. Nothing, therefore, could be done except order the usual tough fare that one expects on such occasions in India, and which is dignified with the name of dinner, to be got ready, and to inspect the arrangements by which mine host proposed to enable me to sleep through the stifling night; for it was hot, very hot, and still. No breeze stirred the leaves of the great trees by which the place was surrounded; instead of the soothing rustle of foliage, the singing of myriads of mosquitoes greeted the ear with a sound of triumph which must have meant that the net bed-curtains in this hotel were no match for them!

Soon, therefore, after eating as much as I could of the

poor repast prepared for me, I decided to retire to rest inside the bedroom, which had, of course, all the doors and windows open, and was furnished with a punkah over the bed, the edge of which passed and re-passed within an inch of my nose, as it was pulled throughout the night by relays of coolies hired for that purpose. In vain did my winged assailants charge pertinaciously at the sleeping form of their intended victim; they were always beaten off by the punkah before they had time to settle, and I passed a more refreshing night than could have been expected with the thermometer over ninety.

Early the next morning I set out sight-seeing, and was soon in the presence of that miracle in white marble—the Taj. This edifice has been so often described, and every one is so familiar with pictures and models of it, that I cannot suppose the reader would care for any lengthy description of it in these pages. I passed a very enjoyable hour in and around this tomb of the Empress Noor Jehan. The garden was well shaded, principally with cypress trees, whose dark foliage contrasted very well with the white marble building. There were also many beds of loquot trees, which grow to a height of twenty or thirty feet. Their fruit was ripe at the time of my visit, and by far the finest of the sort I had ever seen. Many years of cultivation, together with a bountiful and never-failing supply of water, had produced a fruit which only resembled in name any other loquots that I had ever eaten.

On entering the Taj, you are at once accosted by a family of native cicerones. I always patronize this much-abused class, as I will not take the trouble to read up for months before visiting a celebrated place. For two or three florins (rupees), these people were prepared to impart all the information I was likely to require without any trouble to myself. The first thing they presented me with was a small pamphlet containing two criticisms on the Taj, written by men by whom the multitude have decided to be guided. Unfortunately for the multitude, these two gentlemen express diametrically opposite opinions. The first called it the finest building in the world. If he had said the finest tomb, I suppose he could not have been contradicted. The second critic asserts that it is without architectural merits, is only veneered with marble, and that it should have apertures to admit the daylight. With this latter proposition I fully agree. Apertures filled with perforated marble would in no way war with the tomb-like character of the building. Besides, it must be remembered that the remains of the emperor and empress are in a subterranean vault, to which you descend by a narrow staircase. Darkness, however, reigns in the interior of the Taj, with this result, that your guides have to ignite 'blue lights' to enable you to see the decorations, which are really of marvellous beauty and costliness.

The walls, and the monuments of the two departed monarchs, are richly and profusely bejewelled with mosaic-work of such stones as jade, onyx, jasper, cornelian, agate, etc. The shading of the leaves and flowers, and their smoothness, are equal to what one would expect in a lady's brooch; yet each tiny piece is embedded deeply in the marble blocks of which the walls are composed. Such work may court inspection under the brightest rays of the sun; the blue lights, even at their best, only give a dim notion of the reality. The chief guide is aware of this, so he produces promptly from the recesses of his clothing a candle-end, which he lights and holds close to a beautifully-executed design of a full-blown rose about life-size. 'See,' he says 'in this rose alone there are thirty-seven pieces.' I cannot help thinking it a pity that this is not illuminated by the light of day, as similar work is in the palace at Delhi, with such splendid effect.

I never expected to return to this neighbourhood, or to see the Taj by moonlight. Two years later, however, duty took me to Agra for three days. It was lucky that during this short visit the moon was at the full, and I timed my visit so as to arrive in front of the building when the orb of night was high in the heavens, and never shall I forget the beauty of the scene. At such an hour the voice of even the most adverse critic must, I should think, be silenced.

The domed pile of white marble gleamed mysteriously in the moonlight, which at the same time greatly increased the massive darkness of the surrounding cypress trees, above which it towered. Altogether its appearance was now most striking, and I should suppose quite unique. Though it shone so brightly, yet its exact form could not be distinctly discerned. Its size and distance from the spectator seemed to vary with the mood of his own imagination, thus imparting to the structure something of movement as though some huge phantom stood before him in the deep stillness of the night. Alas! that one could only people such a transcendent scene with the dark spectres of a semi-barbarous race.

As soon as my first visit to the Taj was accomplished, I went to see the ruins of the ancient palace of the Mogul emperors, situated about a mile lower down the stream, and on the same bank of the river Jumna.

Hitherto, of all the numerous architectural remains that I had seen in India, not one seemed to convey the idea of any one ever having lived splendidly within them. Solid and heavy blocks of masonry made to match the rocky eminences that they crowned, might, even in the near distance, call up visions of Windsor Castle. I remember being somewhat thus impressed by the templed heights of Parbutty, as I approached them on my way to Poona from Bombay, before the introduction of the railway. As I had then been only forty-eight hours in the country, I was not in a position to make any inquiries of the driver of my vehicle. But the nearer I got, the less it looked like the residence of the governor, which I had at first naïvely supposed it must be. In point of fact, it consisted chiefly of small huts, built with large massive stones, and joined together by walls of the same material. Then very wide flights of steps had been cut out of the natural rock from the bottom to the top of the hill, which, I should think, might be two or three hundred feet above the plain traversed by the high road. All the little coignes of vantage on the lower slopes would have something or other built upon them.

The reader can imagine the fine effect of such decorated hills in the distance, and the disappointment caused by a nearer inspection. The palace at Agra, however, not only equalled, but even in its ruined state surpassed, all that I had ever pictured to myself of Eastern magnificence. The vast courtyard, and all the lofty apartments opening into it, were entirely of polished white marble. But even if I had the technical knowledge and power of description necessary to place before the mental vision of my readers this splendid residence as it now exists, they would still fail to realize to themselves what it must have been like when occupied by a rich and luxurious race of kings.

What would the inhabitants of the cold north think of a habitation in which many fine rooms are without fire-places, doors, or windows? There is ample air and light, for one side of the apartment is often quite open to the outer air, being simply spanned by a finely-moulded arch. Privacy was no doubt secured, and the temperature moderated as required, by rich curtains and silken screens.

During eight months of the year splendid moonlight nights can be relied upon almost with certainty, besides which the native Indians are adepts at illuminations. The fancy can therefore depict without much difficulty the beautiful and regal appearance the large quadrangle must have presented when the great Mogul chose to hold high revel within its precincts. The apartments opened on to a broad walk of white marble, raised about two feet above the level of the court, and perhaps twenty feet in width, on which the upper ten could promenade and view the festivities without being hustled by the crowd. At the back of this again would be the apartments thrown open, and brilliantly illuminated. The whole of this, as I have said before, is in polished white marble, and some of the apartments were entirely overlaid with a bold design executed in gold leaf and other brilliant colours.

Such was the palace as it appeared to me when I viewed it some ten years ago. I had then no intention of writing an account of it. The well-informed reader will therefore, I hope, not be severe if I have described some of the details incorrectly. Indeed, to deal seriously with these grand ruins would doubtless require a book of considerable size, devoted to that subject alone. I shall therefore now say adieu to Agra for ever, and continue on my way to the Terai. The rest of the railway journey presented no features worthy of comment. At Moradabad I found a very nice sort of carriage and pair, with relays every six miles, to take me the next fifty miles of my journey. The horses were good, and always forthcoming without difficulty. The road itself, too, was such as to raise it far above the competition of the best highways I had ever seen in the Bombay Presidency. In addition to being well metalled, it was of great width; on each side ran a turf track as wide as an ordinary English cartway, whilst the centre road would have enabled four carriages to drive abreast. The whole of these three roads throughout the entire length of fifty miles was completely shaded by the branches of the gigantic forest trees that had been planted as an avenue on each side. Their boughs never failed to meet at a great height overhead. Though the rays of the sun would struggle fitfully through the leaves, thinned as they were by the drought and heat of the season, still the shade was such as to enable me actually to enjoy the long drive, instead of performing it under a constant threat of heat apoplexy, as would have been the case on a treeless road.

At a place called Kaladonghi I had to exchange this comfortable mode of travelling for the back of an aged pony with long white hair. This animal had a high character given him in all sincerity by his late owner, of whom I had purchased him for three pounds. He had even received my own Christian name as a mark of distinction. As, on mounting him, there was about an hour of daylight left, and the distance I had to accomplish upon him was under twenty miles, I proposed to make the most of the short time before darkness set in, by setting off at a brisk pace. The track was rough with stones, and there were a good many steep places to go up and down. At the outset, I found the paces of 'Julius' to be not quite what I fancied as the best. 'Could that be a stumble?' I said to myself every time he made an awkward lurch. 'No, no,' I added, 'it is only his method of going; confidence is all that is required,' and I continued to urge my wild career. I had not, however, gone more than two miles before I found myself lying at the bottom of a nullah with Julius on the top of me. I was not hurt, but my confidence was completely destroyed; so, as I had not undertaken this very long and expensive trip for the sake of having a joint sprained or a bone broken, I decided to finish the journey at a foot's pace, and did not arrive at my destination till ten o'clock at night.

Both the pony and I were glad when this tiresome ride was over. A most hospitable welcome awaited us, so that the tedium we had endured for the last four or five hours was forgotten, or only remembered to enhance the enjoyment of better times.

At the time of my arrival I found my friend, in whose hands were all the arrangements for the shooting, unable, through business engagements, to make a start for ten days to come. This period I employed in making the acquaintance of the elephants and their mahouts, informing myself of the manner in which tiger-shooting in these parts was conducted, and finally in exploring the near jungle on the chance of meeting with a newly-arrived tiger. My friend was such a very good shot and keen sportsman, that there were no old settlers of this description anywhere in his vicinity. But as the jungle was very well suited to big game, there was always a possibility of falling in with some new-comers.

The name of the place at which I was now stopping was Ramnugger. It was not exactly in the Terai, but in the border country, called, I believe, the Bābur. Here the Himalayas commence, and although the notable ranges are still far distant, still the land is mountainous, rugged, and wild in the extreme. There is every sort of cover in abundance, from mountains covered with jungle and gashed with ravines, to swamps filled with long grass and dense rushes. Here, as well as in the low-lying belt of the Terai itself, nature was on such a scale as to render a man on foot useless. The beating can only be done by a line of elephants, and even these huge creatures seem dwarfed by the vast surroundings. I have never heard of any rajah, or other great personage, undertaking tiger-shooting in this part of the world with less than forty of these animals. Sometimes hundreds even are mustered for the occasion. Each member of the shooting party is accommodated with an elephant bearing a howdah, in the centre of which he stands in a commanding position, while the mahout drives, protected in front by the fire of the gun, and from behind by the howdah itself.

The main body of the elephants are only furnished with a sort of coarse mattress, secured by ropes bound round the body of the animal. These are used for beating only, and are called pad-elephants. It is very dangerous for any one to make use of one of these animals to shoot from, for should the beast take fright, and make a sudden movement, there is nothing to save a man with a gun in his hand from being thrown off. A friend of mine was killed in this way whilst shooting in the Neemuch jungles. The elephant made a sudden lurch, and the unfortunate man was thrown into the jaws of the wounded tiger, and he received such severe wounds that he died of them in a few days. For beating purposes they do very well, for if there should be any natives besides the mahout on the animal's back, they can always cling on to the ropes, etc., with their hands.

Tiger-shooting in the Terai is best pursued in the months of January and February. In these latitudes it is the cold instead of the heat that causes the thinning of the jungle. This state of things is most propitious to the English sportsman, and does away with the only drawback to the amusement, namely the intense heat, which in every other part of India must be endured by those who would shoot big game. I, however, could only get leave for April and May, at which time of the year the new grass has grown a good deal, and the great heat of the sun acting on the swampy soil is supposed to render the jungle unfit to be entered by Europeans. Indeed, many of my friends, when they were told of my plans, pronounced them to be madness. But I had heard this form of denunciation so often, that I no longer heeded it.

Owing to all the elephants having already had their annual turn of shikar work, my friend was only able to procure seven for our use—two with howdahs, and five with pads. They were kindly lent to us by His Highness the Rajah of Rampore. Three were especially told off for my friend and leader, whilst I, with much satisfaction, took over the other four.

With so small a line, of course, we did not expect to make a large bag. But enjoyment, not fame, was our object, and we were fully resolved to be pleased. I did not want to use the howdah except in jungle where a lower elevation would render shooting impossible. It was agreed, therefore, that I might drive any one of the four committed to my care. I was therefore most congenially occupied during our enforced delay in trying these animals, and making the acquaintance of the mahouts and under-keepers. As the elephants play such an important part in the following narrative, it may interest my readers to know the names of them and their attendants:—

1. Muaruk Guj—mahout, Wazzeer Khan.
2. Indoor Pari, „ Fydeli Khan.
3. Bijli, „ Nunnee.
4. Belculli, „ Iniaz Khan.
5. Noor Jehan, „ Janbaz Khan.
6. Buddul Pyaree, „ Hussein Khan.
7. Chumbeli, „ Goolam Mahomed.

All were elephants of high character and great value. I understood them to be worth three or four hundred pounds each. They were all warranted neither to run away when they winded a tiger, nor to charge a wounded enemy. This latter qualification, however estimable in itself, was not what I liked myself. Tastes are allowed to differ! Among the whole seven there was no large veteran male tusker, such as Roghanath Guj, on whom I could bestow all the affection of which I am capable. All were females except one, Muaruk Guj, and he was without tusks, and not nearly full grown. Yet, in virtue of his sex, I selected him as the special favourite which I would drive myself; whilst Indoor Pari, a female much larger and more powerful than himself, would carry the howdah into which I was destined sometimes to get.

But for the natural impatience to get down into the Terai, and commence shikar in real earnest, the ten days spent at Ramnugger would in themselves have constituted a delightful pic-nic. A few days after my arrival a regiment was halted in the neighbourhood, and the officers all joined in a day's beating on the elephants. We saw no large animals, but it was a wonderful sight to watch the elephants working. The way they got through deep swamps, and over almost precipitous declivities, was astonishing to any one who had only seen them used on roads, or even in moderately broken ground. Having got among the mountains, the leading mahout intimated that we were coming to an awkward-looking pass, but that there was no danger in traversing it. We were heading for an immense yellow rock, perhaps a thousand feet in height, that jutted out into the air, and seemed effectually to block the way. A narrow ledge, however, gradually became visible, which did not look more than three feet wide, and could not have been more than twice that width. It actually overhung the abyss which lay beneath us at a sheer depth of many hundred feet. On to this narrow pathway the leading elephant at once advanced, and was unhesitatingly followed by all the others in single file. The sagacity and nerve of these creatures must be very great, as not one of them seemed the least moved, although their bodies really seemed to bulge over the precipice. About midway, a distance of say thirty or forty yards, the cliff ran out to so sharp an angle that the narrow track round the corner could only be divined, not seen, and the narrow ledge we were upon seemed to run into space. No doubt all this was quite safe, but still I should think it must have been a trying passage for the elephants. On rounding this sort of headland, the same narrow path soon brought us again on to the ordinary steep side of the mountains, and we reached home without meeting with any more striking sights.

In this neighbourhood there were a great many streams of very pure water, forming deep pools at frequent intervals. Owing, I believe, to the protection of the commissioner, the fine fish known as the mahseer was most abundant, and at this time of the year, when the water is as clear as crystal, they can be seen swimming about in all directions, and varying in size from the small fry, too minute to be weighed, to fishes weighing quite fifty pounds. The big ones are very wary, and difficult to take, whilst the little ones are full of rash confidence, and will come in shoals to the surface to scramble for bread crumbs or parched grain. Some being required for breakfast, I fired a bullet into the crowd, and secured five at one shot. I did not weigh them, but they were sufficient to make a good dish for three people.

The next day I took a ride on the elephant Muaruk Guj, and went over some very difficult ground. In one reedy swamp we came on the tracks of a herd of wild elephants, but there was no chance of seeing the animals themselves, for this time, owing to the heat, they migrate to higher regions. A large stag sambur, however, rushed from this cover, and offered a fine broadside shot on the heights above me. I fired, and away the animal went at full speed. We tried to track it, but there was not a vestige of any blood, and it was quite decided that I had missed it. So we mounted our elephants again, and pursued our original line of march, which was to follow the stream that wound round the base of the hill over which the stag had disappeared. After proceeding about a mile we came suddenly on the beast lying quite dead with his nose in the water. The bullet had pierced him just behind the shoulder, and must have gone within an inch or two of the heart, which it may even have touched.

At last came the long-wished-for day for starting on our expedition into the Terai. Our servants, tents, and, in fact, a complete establishment had been sent on overnight. We had only to mount our horses, ride out, and find everything ready for a bath, and breakfast. Even at this, our first halting-place, the appearance and nature of the country was so different to every other part of India that I had ever seen before, that I cannot refrain from endeavouring to give such of my readers as may not have been there some idea of what it was like; indeed, without some description of this peculiar forest tract, it would be impossible for those who had never been there to understand the nature of the sport which I am about to chronicle.

The Terai is a long and narrow belt of country running

along the foot of the Himalayas. It is quite flat, and must receive an immense quantity of water in the way of drainage from the vast range of mountains above it. The soil is black in colour, and of great depth. During the rainy months the whole of this vast district must be under water. It is divided by the inhabitants into localities where they can or can not live through the year. Vast numbers of settlements are regularly abandoned at the approach of the monsoon, and only re-occupied about the beginning of November, when the people return with their great herds of horned cattle for the sake of the grazing. Malaria must be the normal state of the atmosphere. Such a land could only be peopled by a race who, in the course of many generations, have gradually become acclimatized, and have almost ceased to be as other men. I was assured that when any coolies (porters) were employed to carry things up to the station of Nynee Tāl, they always so arranged as to get down the mountain and into the swamp again before nightfall; for them to sleep in the exquisitely clear and bracing air of the mountains, would be extremely dangerous. The drinking water in the Terai is generally looked upon by Europeans as poisonous; but in this I think they are mistaken. Here, as elsewhere through my extensive wanderings, I made it a rule to drink copiously of whatever water the natives were using, and always, I must say, with the best effect. I neither filtered, boiled, nor put anything into it; but I was careful to find out if it really was what the natives themselves were thriving upon. With this proviso, I always would say that the worst water was better for you than the best wine. When exposed all day long to the fierce rays of a May sun, it is a good thing to drink as much as possible, for the sake of promoting that perspiration which alone keeps you from catching fire; and I think it is only of simple water that you can take a sufficient quantity for this purpose. A mixture of any other fluid, when drunk so profusely of, is sure to disorder the health of any one who is not unusually strong. There is, no doubt, much difficulty in such a rotten soil in keeping the wells open, and they are often lined with a sort of brushwood that imparts a very disagreeable flavour to the water; but still I found from experience that even this did not make the contents of the well unwholesome. It may be asked how in a flat country full of water wells could be sunk, and what should be the necessity for them? To this I would answer, that no doubt it must be difficult to find a level sufficiently high to admit of the necessary sinking, and that water, taken from the endless, slow, sluggish streams that flow with a scarcely perceptible movement through the dense reeds and grass with which the face of the earth is covered, really might be poisonous unless it were subjected to a certain amount of percolation.

Of course, though all is flat to the eye, there must be considerable variations in the level, as is shown by the frequent occurrence of terrible swamps, called 'fassands' by the natives. In these even an elephant may be engulphed in a moment. All is, however, covered with a mantle of grass eight feet high, and so dense that when a herd of the smaller deer or pig get confused, and run back on the line, it is quite impossible to see what sort of animals are on foot, though they are so close that the elephants have to stamp and kick to keep them off their legs. Yet the number of the creatures can be pretty well guessed at, as each in its flight produces an effect on the herbage as if a narrow whirlwind were traversing its surface. The only animal that I could ever see under such circumstances was the large yellow swamp deer, which would go off with a succession of high leaps, by means of which he could see and be seen. Even tigers can only be viewed by following them till chance, or skill in driving, causes them to cross some spot where the cover, from some temporary reason, is thin enough to expose them partially to view. The rule is, not to fire at the moving grass, but to wait in hopes of getting at least a glimpse of the animal. Wherever one is on this great plain of grass, the horizon seems bounded by a dark line of huge trees, which generally turn out to be a narrow strip, and not thickly planted. Sometimes, however, it proves to be the border of a large forest, and is full of all kinds of vegetation; stinging nettles, for instance, grow in large patches, and so high that they reach above the heads of the elephants, who are so much hurt by the pungency of this weed that some become quite ungovernable through it, and all cordially detest working in it. These forests are called 'bojees' by the natives, and are not quite so characteristic of the Terai as the great grass plains previously described.

CHAPTER IX.

BHINKERI was the name of the small hamlet from which we made our first start. The grass here was reckoned long and thick even for the Terai, so it was arranged that on this occasion I should stand in the howdah borne by the large female elephant Indoor Pari. Immediately on leaving the grove of trees occupied by the little settlement, and in and around which the herbage was beaten down, we found ourselves in a sort of wide ocean of pale-green grass reaching up to the elephants' backs. Large, dark mango trees grew either singly or in straggling lines, and looked, I thought, not unlike rocks projecting from the sea. We did not expect to get any sport here, as a large party had just preceded us, and had killed three large tigers. The natives, however, assured us that there was at least one left, for they could not only hear it, but their cattle were still being killed by one of these beasts.

The head man of the village was placed on an elephant, and acted as guide, and we were soon launched on to this great strange-looking plain. Of course, owing to the grass, not a living thing could be seen; and one can only still wonder how even the oldest inhabitant contrives to form any conjecture as to the probable whereabouts of anything that has the power of locomotion. Perhaps the tigers attach themselves to the herds over whom they exercise a close and dreadful surveillance. Be this as it may, we had not proceeded far when the apparently lifeless solitude was cheered by the sound of a human voice calling out lustily from the midst of a detached and distant mango tree. We at once steered our ships in the required direction. On approaching the tree, we found ourselves in the midst of a herd of tame buffaloes, who were being guarded in some mysterious and, I should think, quite futile manner by the poor fellow in the tree. Notwithstanding the monotony of the landscape, he was able, by means of certain trees, long strips of discoloured grass, and such-like marks, to indicate the favourite resting-place of his terrible enemy. He summed up by saying, 'If he is not between us and that curved line of mango trees, he must have left the neighbourhood altogether for the present, and it will be useless to look for him to-day.'

Acting on this information, we proceeded with our search, and before we had got fairly clear of the great tame buffaloes, the grass was seen to be moving in a swift and stealthy manner, which even I could see at a glance was not caused by one of the herd of cattle. We at once formed a line, and followed the moving grass. The tiger could not know that all was safe in any direction he might choose, and would therefore proceed cautiously till, owing to some undulation in the ground, or the herbage being trampled by the herds, he could obtain a view of his foes. And it was precisely as he was passing along a track made by the buffaloes that I caught a sight of him. I took a rapid shot with my No. 12 smooth-bore gun, and planted a bullet sufficiently near the heart to disable him. He charged at once among the elephants, and the mahouts all shouted in chorus, 'Māro! māro!' *i.e.* 'Kill him! kill him!' This we were not slow to do. He received a volley from our three guns as he came rushing on, and died almost at the foot of my elephant, without having done any damage. This proved to be a splendid male animal, and measured longer than any I have ever seen killed. His length as he lay on the ground before us was nine feet eleven inches.

At the next place we came to there seemed to be no tigers among the grass, so we made for a wood or bojee that appeared in the distance. On our way to it we had to cross many of the sluggish streams I have before spoken of. The banks are generally quite perpendicular, but the water is seldom more than two or three feet deep, so that if the bottom is sound there is no difficulty in the passage.

The men of the district whom you have with you know pretty well the nature of the soil, and they are always consulted before making the plunge. As they have no elephants of their own, they do not always know what effect the heavy weight of one of these animals may have on the slimy bottom of the watercourse. That they may sometimes prove mistaken was shown in crossing one of these places on this occasion, for no sooner had Indoor Pari got well into the water than she sank deep into the mire. Her distress was painful to witness; the more she kneaded the mud, the deeper she found herself planted therein, till at last the water reached nearly up to the bottom of the howdah. We all got off, keeping well clear of her trunk, for under such desperate circumstances they will use this limb to catch hold of anything that may come within their reach, which they will work underneath them to form an artificial footing. If they can be supplied with plenty of materials for this purpose, they will not be long in extricating themselves. But, even if we had been sufficiently devoted to offer our bodies for this purpose, our numbers were not enough to be of any use. We therefore stood on the bank, and, on looking attentively, we could see that amid her rolling and groaning she was making a little way. Her struggles ended in her getting herself out, at which, of course, we were all very glad.

Nothing further occurred till we got into the bojee, where the hunting was very interesting. The woods were full of jungle fowl. The little red cocks were flying about in all directions, looking and crowing like bantams, till one could have imagined oneself in a farmyard. One little dark hen was in a dreadful fuss. She had a brood of small chickens about the size of reels of cotton. How to prevent the elephants from putting their feet on to one or more of these treasures was a question that no amount of screaming and fluttering, with outspread wings, would solve. If any were killed, some no doubt escaped, and she would not notice the diminished number. After being in the bojee a short time I heard the report of a gun, and found that my friend had shot a panther; but I do not remember that any adventure was connected with the destruction of this animal.

Up to this time we were a party of three, and the day after the events described above a very fine panther was shot by the sportsman who had hitherto been unlucky.

It was an unusually large panther, and measured eight feet two inches in length. I only remember to have seen one that exceeded this measurement. It was eight feet three inches from nose to tip of tail. Yet even this latter quadruped could easily, when slung on a pole, be carried by two men, whilst a tigress of no greater length would require to be laid on a litter, with eight or ten men as bearers. In short, the tiger and the panther are very different animals.

After this our party was reduced to two in number, as our third man had only been able to obtain short leave of absence. I think it was the day after he left us, that we had very good grounds for believing that a tigress had taken up her quarters in a ravine that was deep for that part of the country. We determined to get into trees on this occasion, and send away the elephants, so that the tigress might not be driven back by seeing them in front of her. At my station there was only a small slim sort of stem to get upon, so I drove the elephant up to it, and stepped from his head into the only fork that this little thorn possessed. The mahout then took my place, and backed the elephant from the tree. These beasts, though their sight is very keen, have only a limited field of vision. Muarak Guj had evidently seen nothing of what had gone on over his head, so, when the backing process brought me into view, he evidently mistook me for a gigantic and probably malevolent bear or monkey. The result was that he charged furiously, seized the sapling with his trunk, and bent it with such force that I lost my seat, but held on to a bough with my hands. Though I felt my feet touch the ground, I was afraid to let go, as he would certainly have nipped hold of me, and trampled me to death. He, fortunately, could not break the stem, and when he let go, I flew up again to the original altitude. This was repeated two or three times, always with the same result. I need hardly say the mahout all this time was working might and main, with the ankus, to induce him to desist; but, as in moments of excitement these men always pursue the same tactics, I dare say the poor elephant thought he was being urged on to battle! At last, however, he seemed to understand what he was wanted to do, and retiring, took up his stand about twenty yards off. I then dropped to the ground, and advanced, calling to him by name. He recognized me at once, and in the most friendly manner extended the tip of his trunk for me to step on to, and at once hoisted me on to his head. There I was obliged to sit, as the tree was quite spoilt, and there was no time to make any fresh arrangement. I fear that all this disturbance must have given the tigress warning of our proximity, and enabled her to keep clear of us. At any rate, nothing was seen of her. As it was by no means certain that she was still in this neighbourhood, we shifted our ground the next day to a spot about ten miles distant, where there was a very deep and wide ravine, though I do not think it was of any great length. There was also a good deal of thick forest round about.

My friend having crossed over to the opposite side of the nullah, the pad-elephants formed a line between us, and the usual beat commenced. Almost immediately I heard a roar in the direction of my friend's elephant, and saw the head and shoulders of an immense tiger starting with open jaws from a deep and leafy recess on the opposite side. My friend fired promptly. I happened to be in the howdah on this occasion, where I was supposed to have so much greater facility for shooting than when driving the elephant myself. However, notwithstanding the great distance I was from the tiger, yet its sudden apparition was so formidable, that Indoor Pari endeavoured to bolt before I could get a shot, and the mahout was unable to keep her steady. I could not see Muaruk Guj anywhere, so I made the mahout get inside the howdah with my gun-bearer, Chowpatty, and, driving the elephant myself, I started up the nullah after the tiger. I had got detached from the party, and had been quite alone for so long that I began to despair of finding either my friends or the tiger, when suddenly the latter appeared in front of me presenting, I must say, an easy shot. I fired both barrels, on which he turned and disappeared over a projecting mound. On surmounting this I saw at my feet in a little dell a very thick patch of grass. I felt sure the brute would be in this, and put the elephant into it. She had not advanced two steps when she made a determined halt, showing that she had winded the tiger.

I now debated inwardly whether it would be better to urge the beast, and risk starting the tiger at an unfavourable moment, or whether I should wait quite quietly till the enemy should make up his mind to move, and thus betray his exact whereabouts. My reflections on this head were, however, soon cut short by the most welcome appearance of my friend, borne by his favourite elephant, Noor Jehan, on the opposite bank, just above where the tiger was lying. I called out, and asked him kindly to stop, as I felt sure

Indoor Pari would advance firmly across the grass to join her friends, who were now all assembled on the opposite side. I was right in this conjecture; but she had no real pluck, for the moment the tiger jumped up in front of her, she wheeled round like lightning, and before I had time to fire, was crashing, at her best double-shuffle, through the thick adjacent forest. I did my best to guide her, and contrived to keep the howdah clear of any such large boughs and limbs of trees as would have been fatal to it. Still, the treatment it received was very severe, and the two inhabitants were having a truly wretched time of it. They both took refuge under the seat, and continually cried, 'Arè Bāba! Arè Bāba!' which means, 'Oh, my Father!'

This stampede did not last more than two or three hundred yards, but considering that every step was through a strong tree jungle, it was really a marvel that the howdah was still on the elephant's back when she drew up. I am sure when elephants are flying terror-stricken, it is much better not to attempt to stop them at once, but to be satisfied with guiding them till they are a bit blown, and think themselves out of danger.

I now had to retrace my steps as quickly as possible, to assist in the further operations of the chase. I was not long in coming up with the rest of the party, who had ringed the tiger on a small islet in the centre of one of the sluggish mud-bottomed streams common to this country. He was in such a dense patch of cover that there seemed no chance of his moving, so there was time to call a halt and discuss our future measures. The first thing I did was to call up Muaruk Guj, and get off Indoor Pari, with the inward resolve never to mount her again. Chowpatty and his friend emerged from under a heap of leaves and sticks, and the edifice itself was so battered that it had to be sent to the maker's for repair, but he said nothing could be done to it; so henceforth I felt I need have nothing more to do with howdahs. I was not sorry, for whatever may be said as to the advantages of superior height, etc., for getting the shot, I find it much more amusing to drive myself. Having got on to the neck of the male elephant, I felt quite at home, and was prepared to cross the stream and enter the 'eyot' at once. But the natives of the place, many of whom had come with us on the pad-elephants, were unanimous in pronouncing that the bottom of this channel was a 'fasand,' or bottomless bog. This was such a serious complication that I looked around to see what else could be done, and I observed a long, thin tree growing on our bank, and leaning right over the rushes on the other side. From the head of the elephant I got into this tree, and climbed till I overhung the opposite side. Then was apparent the excitability and nervousness of Asiatics. They all called out, 'Kubburdār! Kubburdār!' 'Take care! take care! the roots of the tree are giving way!' I was not, however, the least alarmed, as I felt that it was quite firm, notwithstanding the rottenness of the bank in which it was growing. It was lucky for me that it stood firm, for the sharp eyes of the tiger had detected me, or perhaps his ears directed him; at all events, he charged close under me, but for some reason or other did not spring, and then rushed back in the same swift and silent manner.

During this manœuvre he remained quite invisible, only

the waving grass betrayed his actions; so, remembering the rule for such occasions, I refrained from firing, and, as it was evident I never should see him, situated as I was, I again got on to the head of the elephant. The tiger now lay very quiet, and nothing that we could find to throw in seemed to affect him. We therefore decided to make an exception to the rule, and fire into the grass, even though we could see nothing. At the first shot he began to rush about the little island, and we fired many times without knowing what the result might have been. Finally, the animal made a rush just to the brink of the water, and then moved no more. We could make nothing out with any certainty, so I decided at last to put Muaruk Guj into the stream, on the chance that the bottom might bear him. Considering the positive statements of the natives, I was surprised to find that it afforded a good footing, so I proceeded with confidence to the edge of the stream, where we felt sure the tiger was lying. Arrived at this point, I suddenly turned the elephant into the dense grass and rushes, expecting him to step up out of the water. Instead of that his leg sank up to the shoulder in the swamp, out of which all this herbage was growing, and his head projected into the rushes to within a few feet of the hidden enemy. The position was most critical, but the elephant was fully equal to the occasion. Instead of floundering forward, he at once sat down in the water where the ground was firm behind him. Then he carefully wriggled his entangled leg till he got it underneath him, and rose again to his full height.

I must say I felt considerably relieved to find myself once more in comparative safety. But the problem of how to bag this tiger seemed further than ever from being satisfactorily solved, when, quite unexpectedly, a man who had climbed to a great height up an adjacent forest tree, announced that he could see a portion of the tiger's body. He proceeded to cut or break off pieces of thickish twigs, and succeeded, he said, in letting them fall actually on to the recumbent beast. But it stirred not, neither did it utter any sound. We therefore thought it must be dead, and agreed to go in together on foot, with our guns, I need hardly say, at full cock. Crossing the stream where it would bear the elephants, we got to the other side of the island, where a fallen tree of great size lay prone, and forming a footway almost up to where the animal was concealed. Here we dismounted, and walked along the fallen trunk, till we came suddenly on the brute, which really was quite dead, fortunately for us. It was a very handsome tiger, and of unusual size, though not very long, measuring not more than 9 feet 9½ inches; but it was of great bulk and weight. Happening to make some remark about it to one of the leading natives, whilst we were trying to get it on to the elephant's back, he exclaimed, 'It is indeed a fine large beast. Why, here we are, eighteen men with ropes, and it seems as if we should never get it on to Belculli's back.'

Of course, before loading it on the elephant, we carefully inspected the carcase to see which of us had killed it. At first it seemed as if it had died out of mere politeness; not a single wound could be found. At last, however, in the loose skin behind the ears, just at the base of the skull, the hide was seen to be cut. A bullet had passed through this unobtrusive hole, and had killed this magnificent beast on the spot. There was just a little curled shaving of lead found in the wound, that evidently belonged to one of my friend's Express bullets; so his were the honours of this chase, which I think we both enjoyed equally.

On getting back to our tents, the tiger was unloaded from the elephant's back in the centre of a little clearing in the forest, to leeward of the camp, and the usual business of skinning was proceeded with. As I stood watching the proceedings, I noticed even more than the usual number of great vultures assembling on the surrounding trees, anxiously waiting for the banquet, which experience told them would soon be theirs. Directly the carcase, stripped of its skin, and therefore no longer an object of terror, was left, they all descended upon it in a cloud, and nothing could be seen but a large heaving mass of feathers, round which two jackals kept trotting humbly, and wagging their little short tails. They were not, however, suffered to pick up even the smallest scrap. The vultures took no notice whatever of them, but I suppose if they had ventured to interfere they would have been set upon and killed. I looked at my watch as the first bird alighted on the body of the tiger, and found that in exactly twenty minutes these feathered scavengers had so completely done their work that there was nothing but a skeleton left. With the exception of a little sinewy flesh about the paws, the bones exactly resembled those of another tiger which we knew had been exposed for more than a month. Indeed, except that the bones were in both cases not bleached white, these skeletons might have lain there for years as far as appearances went. The dressing of this large skin unfortunately exhausted my stock of arsenical soap, and it was only after some delay, and a good deal of trouble, that we could get more of this composition forwarded to us. In the hot climate of India much care must be taken with the skins of the beasts you shoot, if you wish them to be worth the expense of bringing to England, and expect them to be a credit to you when mounted. It is quite a mistake to suppose that a clever London naturalist can, by his art, make an ill-used skin look as well as a perfect one. An experienced eye will at once detect every flaw, and, after the article has been for a short time in use, nothing else but the patching, painting, etc., will be noticed, even by the most casual observer. The very first thing to be done is to pull out the tiger's whiskers, secure them in a piece of rag or paper, and put them in your pocket. The natives, as I think I have already stated, burn these ornamental bristles, from motives either of ignorance or superstition. Notwithstanding that I always carefully preserved these capillary treasures, and duly handed them over to the artist with the skins, I found that he had substituted in the heads the ribs of birds' feathers with the web stripped off. By this plan your trophy can be whiskered to an alarming extent, and comes home looking magnificent. The extreme readiness with which they became limp, and even broke off, caused me to inspect them carefully, and I thus made the above discovery.

Having then secured the bristles, and plentifully anointed the thick parts, such as the lips, head, ears, and paws, with arsenical soap on both sides, it should be pegged out symmetrically, and not too tightly, in a place where no sun can reach it. If too much stretched, it may burst, and if the sun be allowed to shine on it, the fat melts and fills the inside of each hair, which is a hollow tube, and the brightness of the fur is thus tarnished beyond all possibility of remedy. As soon as the hide is properly laid out, some of the villagers are employed at once to rub in wood-ashes by means of small pieces of brick, which are hard, and yet will not cut the skin. By this process all the flesh is gradually rubbed off, and whatever fat may be left in the animal's coat is thoroughly deoderized by the ashes, which must be the residuum of wood, and not of coal or other mineral substance.

With relays of labourers a skin can be prepared quite well in one night, and rendered fit for packing.

A day or two after killing this large tiger, another, said to be quite his equal, was reported to be occupying some very long grass near the borders of a forest. We journeyed consequently to a small hamlet in the vicinity, but arrived too late to shoot that day. Towards evening, and throughout the night, we were cheered by the strange nervous clacking noise made, I know not how, by the spotted deer, when rendered anxious by the known presence of their redoubtable oppressor. From this we augured well for the morrow's sport.

Accordingly, the next day we started in good time. I rode Muaruk Guj, in whose courage both I and his mahout had begun to place as much confidence as was possible, considering he had never been tried by an actual combat with a tiger. He was young, not full grown, and without tusks, so I felt almost remorseful when urging him into danger. But there was no more suitable animal to be obtained, so I was obliged to risk him. The mahout laid great stress on his having tried to pull me out of the tree, as I have already recounted, and on another occasion he had charged at a wild pig, kicking with his foot as though playing at football. 'From these circumstances,' said Wazzeer Khan, 'I think he certainly means fighting.'

Sending the mahout on another elephant, I hung two guns round my neck, and did my very best to hit off the track of the tiger. All at once my elephant began kicking with his front legs, and looked highly excited. The grass in front, by its sinuous and snake-like movement, betrayed the tiger making his retreat. Unfortunately the grass was so thick that I could not see him at all till he had got thirty yards off, and even then I only got a glimpse of him going at a swift pace. I fired both barrels of my gun, on which he roared and disappeared like a flash of lightning. I had wounded him, as we could track him by his blood, but owing to the dense and extensive nature of the jungle, we never saw him again. The only wonder is how anything that once gets out of sight in these regions can ever be recovered. In this case we had unfortunately omitted to have the high trees manned with scouts. If this precaution had been taken, we might very possibly have secured this prize.

We were destined, however, to be soon consoled for this piece of bad luck. The next day, at a place called Buksora, we were beating through long grass in the usual manner, when a tigress was seen to raise her head over the cover at some distance in front of us. We immediately took up as long a line as possible, and pushed on in pursuit. Before long I heard the report of my friend's rifle, which was quickly followed by the appearance of a very fine tigress galloping across a small opening about fifty yards from me. I fired, and the bullet took such good effect that she stopped her flight, and dashed into a near tract of the densest cover she could find. All the seven elephants were immediately urged in every direction, to try and discover her retreat. At last I heard distant shouts of success. I hurried in the direction of these welcome sounds, but, having wandered rather far a-field, I was the last to arrive near the scene of action, and found everything ready for the final struggle. The six elephants were standing in a scattered line, and the mahouts were all pointing to a circular depression in the ground of about fifty yards in diameter. This was surrounded by a natural embankment surmounted by some vast forest trees. The centre of this little arena was occupied by a swamp, in which the grass and rushes grew in such stifling luxuriance that the trees of the adjacent forest had been unable to advance upon it. It was in the middle of this little dell that the tigress had resolved to make her last stand.

My friend, being much the best shot of the party, was posted in a tree that commanded the whole ground, whilst I, placing myself at the head of the elephants in 'Indian file,' led the way to the lair of the wounded beast. As I approached, I could see the tall herbage shiver, but the swamp was not deep, and there was nothing to impede the march of Muaruk Guj. When at about twenty yards from the tigress, she uttered a short growl, and favoured us with a view of herself in the air, above the grass, with her back arched and tail curled. I fired, but probably missed.

She disappeared for a second, and then with unerring aim hurled herself on to the head of my elephant. Her fangs were buried deep in the soft pads on his crown, where one is wont to prod him with the ankus. I could have touched her muzzle with my hand. I had no weapon but my gun, and she was too close for me to get it up to my shoulder. I had just time to admire the brilliancy of her attack, when I found myself, I know not how, flying through the air in her company. The elephant had given a prodigious shake, and got rid of us both at once. My feet were torn from the kelāwa or neck-band in which the mahout's feet are secured. Many of the strings broke, and some of the eyelet hooks of my boots were torn out at the same time. Yet, strange to say, I was not in the least hurt, and had an eye for all that was going on. For a second I saw myself in the air with the tigress, and almost simultaneously found myself sitting quite comfortably in a nest of long fine grass, within a yard of my infuriated enemy. I knew she was there, for I had received no shock, and had at once listened for her backward rush into the heart of her stronghold. Not the faintest sound of any kind, however, had greeted my attentive ear. The crashing and grunting of the elephants, who had all taken to ungovernable flight through the dense forest, soon ceased to be audible. Not even a bird was twittering in the heat of the mid-day sun. All was silent; there was nothing to disturb my reflections!

Owing to my excellent arrangements beforehand, I was not, even at this desperate crisis, at all uncomfortable. My gun was properly secured round my neck, and hung ready, with the butt in the hollow of the right shoulder. My serviceable sun helmet was secured by a stout chin-strap, and occupied its wonted position on my head. Still, with all these advantages, I felt that my life was really not worth sixpence! I asked myself what I should do. Well, I thought, there can be no harm in loading my one empty barrel. To carry this project into execution, I drew back the trigger so as to avoid making a click on coming to half-cock. I then opened the gun, and took a cartridge out of my pocket. On presenting this at the breech, I suddenly perceived that my hand was shaking like an aspen leaf. At this I felt much vexed, and refused to go on with the loading till it stopped, for, of course, one should not get into such situations if one's hand is going to tremble. Was this the way to justify myself in the eyes of those friends who had earnestly endeavoured to dissuade me from practising the mahout's calling? A moment of such considerations was sufficient to calm me, and I duly placed the bullet in the chamber of the gun. But though I felt quite composed, and was now really able to appreciate the adventure, I felt that my position was as serious as ever. Should it occur to the tigress to scent me, she would make one pounce through the grass, and nothing but a miracle would save me from being torn to pieces. The first move seemed to be the thing to avoid on both sides, so I sat quite still, and listened intently for any sound that would indicate the exact spot occupied by my foe. All, however, remained wrapped in the sultry stillness usual to the locality at this time. The tigress must have suppressed her very breathing whilst listening for the possible return of her enemies.

Several minutes had elapsed since I had been left seated

thus precariously in the grass. I was quite alone, for the tree in which my companion was posted did not command the exact spot where I had fallen, so that we could not see each other, and he was probably under the impression that I was struggling with the refractory Guj in the midst of the banyan jungle. I had just decided to sit immoveable, and let the tigress make the first move, when all the elephants emerged in line from the forest, and formed a row on the bank above me. Instantly I raised my hand straight above my head, and there held it rigidly, as a sign for them to stop. The mahouts at once understood the danger of bearing down on me, and in a moment the elephants all stood solemnly at attention. I rose to my feet, and stood for a moment erect, wondering whether this move might bring me into the view of the glistening yellow eyes that I knew were trying to pierce the dense cover. No, nothing stirred; the screen had evidently stood the test. Close up to where I had been projected into the grass was the narrow pathway which had been trampled down by the advance of the elephants. I felt that if I could gain this track, I should probably be as safe as most people are at any moment of their lives.

The first step was to me one of thrilling interest, for it would doubtless decide my fate. I laid hold of the soft long green grass with both hands, to make a passage for myself out of the sort of nest in which I had found safety. Being full of sap, the stalks parted without making the slightest rustle, and the earth under my feet was damp, and soft as velvet. I could not hear myself move as I cautiously and slowly took the first few steps. I then felt that caution was no longer necessary, and advanced at my usual pace to the line of elephants. Muaruk Guj stood in the centre of them, adorned with a long though not deep scratch down the middle of his trunk. The mahouts all called out to me not to approach him from the front, as in his then excited state he might attack me. But we were such friends by this time, that I felt certain he would be glad to see me.

CHAPTER X.

I THEREFORE advanced towards him with a confidence that was not quite so perfect as it seemed, for these animals, as a rule, when about to trample you, make absolutely no sign of their evil intentions till their victim is within reach. Then they make sure of him! However, on the present occasion, I had every cause to feel pleased with my friend. He received me with evident pleasure, and on my taking hold of his trunk he at once extended the tip of it for me to put my foot on, and conveyed me on to his wounded head as he had always been accustomed to do. A round of applause and congratulations now very naturally burst from the surrounding natives, who must have quite given me up for lost.

'What,' they exclaimed, 'are we to do now?'

'Follow me,' I said, and again descended into the arena on the neck of Muaruk Guj, who seemed to have quite recovered his courage, and led the way with his habitual dignity. As we approached the well-known spot I had just left, again the grass rustled, answering as it were to the uneasy movements of the tigress. But the elephant showed no signs of fear and never checked his stately pace, even when his enemy uttered some low and angry growls. Just as we had got to the very point where the last attack had been made, the tigress made an exactly similar spring, and once more crowned the head of the unfortunate Guj. It was all so swift, there was no possibility of firing with any good effect. I had not even time to urge the elephant to come down on his head, and thus get the tigress under him, and trample her to death. He was too young and inexperienced to execute this manœuvre. He could only repeat his former tactics, and again flung his assailant from him. I can quite believe that he prevented the muscles of his neck from moving in order not to unseat me, as there is no limit to the sagacity and power of these creatures. Certain it is that I felt no difficulty in keeping my place, and consequently I formed one of the flying squadron, who again rushed wildly into the thickest jungle they could find. We all managed to avoid the heavy boughs, either by judicious steering, or by wriggling below the line of the elephant's head and back. On this occasion they went considerably over their ordinary travelling pace of three miles an hour! We were not long in bringing them all to a stand-still, and returning again to where we had left the tigress, against whom I again led the attack. But the elephants were by this time much demoralized, and every time the tigress spoke they wheeled sharp round, and flounced about in dire confusion. Of course, our difficulty consisted in this, that the tigress was, owing to the dense nature of the cover, perfectly invisible till she climbed on to the head of one of the elephants. Our only course, therefore, was to go on charging at the beast, either till it moved, or till we had trampled down all the herbage in which she was lying concealed. With these intentions I urged Muaruk Guj to repeated advances, but whenever he got to within ten yards of the tigress she would roar, and then he would hastily fall back on his female followers, and all would begin the same mad dance. All at once, in the midst of one of these performances, a cry rose of 'Jāta, jāta,' 'she is off,' which was quickly followed by the double report of my friend's rifle. I hastened in pursuit, but now the elephants refused to mount the embankment, or to quit the cover, which they at once knew to be clear of any hostile inhabitant. The men in the trees positively asserted that the tigress was dead, but the elephants evidently knew better, and were most reluctant to advance. I therefore ordered Indoor Pari to advance abreast of my elephant. We then simultaneously delivered a shower of blows and prods on their devoted crowns with the ankus, and shouted our battle cries at the same time. This had the desired effect. The two animals seemed to exchange a glance of intelligence, and then shoulder to shoulder rushed up the slope, and once more set the tigress in motion. Those in the trees could see her as she charged on to the elephant, Noor Jehan, who, however, escaped with only a slight scratch, for the tigress wheeled round and flew towards the hindmost elephant, Buddul Pyaree, whom she seized first by the shoulder, and then fixed on to her hind leg, making her teeth meet through the flesh. This I saw myself through an opening of the trampled herbage. Buddul Pyaree behaved with such masculine courage on this occasion that I was very sorry she was not one of the animals told off for my use. She sat down on her foe, whom she got well under her, and nearly smothered in the mud. All the people on the elephant's pad fell off during this process, and came running up towards the main body. One of them, called Seesoo, had even got a scratch from the tiger's claw on his temple, so he had had a narrow escape. In another second or two, the elephant rose and came rapidly shuffling towards us. The tigress then sat up for an instant blackened with mud, and looking more ferocious than ever. She again disappeared into the very same thicket of rushes whence she had delivered her attacks on me. Of course, we had been firing a good deal during all this time, but the elephants were so unsteady that one could not tell with what result. With much difficulty we succeeded in getting the elephants into this patch of cover, and my friend from the elevation of his howdah discovered her lying dead, but in such a position as to preserve the appearance of life. The mahout, Janbaz Khan, however, threw his ankus deftly on to her back, and she never moved; so, being certain she was dead, I dismounted, and advancing with my gun, aimed at her. I put my foot on her tail. The natives now really believed she was dead. The elephants had been certain of it some short time before, and gathered round their late redoubtable enemy with the utmost indifference. On inspecting the dead animal, we found her pierced with so many wounds that we could not tell what shots had missed or taken effect. Her great vitality had enabled her to bear up against adverse circumstances long after an ordinary beast would have succumbed. She was eight feet eight inches in length, and had a beautifully marked skin.

Naturally, the first thing we did on getting to our tents was to attend to the wounded elephants. Muaruk Guj and Buddul Pyaree were both a good deal hurt, though not seriously. The former had received all his deep wounds about the crown of the head, and his left eye was concealed by a swelling about the size of an ordinary footstool. But as he was already nearly blinded by cataract on that side, this was not of much consequence. Still, he must have been very sore about the head, and it spoke highly for his temper that he had allowed me to climb over his scratched trunk and wounded head when I remounted him in the intervals of the fight. Buddul Pyaree's hind leg and shoulder were deeply wounded, but no flesh had been torn out. I treated both animals by injecting brandy and salt, as I had fortunately brought a glass syringe with me.

I had been cautioned not to go near Buddul Pyaree as she was dangerous, and was not one of those told off for my use. Therefore her conduct when being operated upon was greatly to her credit. She always received me kindly, and bore the stinging pain of the brandy and salt with great patience. It must have hurt her very much, as the flesh for a foot or so all round used to quiver and contract with pain whilst her wounds were being dressed in this way. I often regretted that Buddul Pyaree was not one of my elephants, as she might have turned out a more fighting beast than the young 'mukna,' as the tuskless males are called. I have always found that elephants are very quick to discern your motives. They will put up with any punishment for misconduct, or to cure them of any disease; but wanton ill-treatment, and above all a practical joke, they will often resent by killing the perpetrator of it.

As there was known to be a pair of tigers at this place, we resolved to stay and hunt up the remaining one. For two days, however, we worked without success, but on the third morning we soon heard the old tiger roaring lustily. Hitherto, I suppose, he had been patiently waiting the reappearance of his spouse. At any rate he was on this day exercising some of his finest notes, which he little knew would prove his death-song. Guided by the sounds, we were soon in his vicinity, when, divining that he was pursued, he stopped his concert, and crouched in what he considered a safe nook. And here he might possibly have given us the slip had not all the elephants winded him. I had never seen them do this so well before. They all stood around at different posts, and stretching out their trunks towards a common centre, they pointed unmistakeably to the very spot where the tiger was lying. We all drew gradually in upon him, till, feeling himself surrounded, he tried to rush past my friend, who despatched him with one bullet, and the beast fell dead without uttering a groan. It was a fine tiger, extremely fat, and measured nine feet seven inches.

Our next move was to a very large wood, called the Goolur bojee. Here the jungle was of unusual strength. Everything seemed thrown *pêle mêle* together, — immense trees, dense underwood, with beds of rushes and cane-brakes of great height and thickness. The watercourses had cut deep into the soft soil, making for the unwary traveller many dangerous and treacherous pitfalls; for the whole surface of the land is so covered with grass as to look, wherever there are no trees, like a smooth English hay-field ready for cutting. It was here, I think, that, finding I could only with difficulty get the elephant along, I spoke to the mahout who was sitting behind me. 'Oh,' he said, 'we are in the middle of a large tree that has fallen down.' And such was really the case.

Another very strange effect is experienced when any large portion of the jungle is on fire. I only once met with this on a large scale, and but for the immediate and confident assurance of all present that there was not the slightest danger, I should certainly have thought that there was extreme peril in the conflagration. The cracking of the canes was like the firing of innumerable pistols, and seemed to extend over a large area. The general character of the vegetation, however, is not sufficiently dry and sapless to enable the fire to tear along at speed, and in a general line before the wind. Even the wild animals seem to know that there is no cause for alarm; for though the tracks of several tigers were visible in all directions and quite fresh, yet neither they nor any other beasts appeared to be on the move. But, as far as I remember, this burning jungle was at some distance from the Goolur bojee of which I am now writing.

We saw a very singular sight the first day that we went out in this neighbourhood. I was driving Muaruk Guj on the extreme right of the advancing line, and as I gradually found myself too far to the front, I halted to enable the others to get abreast of me, and could not understand why they were so long in coming up. The delay was soon explained by word being passed to me that a large snake was in the act of gorging a parah stag in the presence of the rest of the party. I hastened to put the elephant across the intervening swamp, and soon arrived at the spot, where a strange spectacle met my gaze.

The elephants were drawn up facing a dense screen of rushes, in front of which, on an open space, lay extended, in a straight and stiffened line, a huge snake. The front part of the beast was tremendously distended, so that it looked exactly like a small beer barrel with a long tail to it. On a nearer inspection the head of the snake could be seen projecting from the thick end, with the two hind feet of the deer sticking out of one corner of its mouth. I was told that when first seen a large portion of the stag's body was still to be seen; but apparently the work of deglutition had proceeded too far to admit of disgorging. It had therefore continued the business of swallowing with such rapidity, that by the time I arrived only the two feet were to be seen. It might, however, just as well have refrained from hurrying itself, and have enjoyed its last meal as long as it could. For there it lay, and seemed likely long to lie, quite helpless, and totally incapable of stirring an inch. We could not shoot this monster for fear of disturbing the tiger, which we hoped might be close at hand. We therefore commanded one of the natives to go and cut its head off. None, however, seemed the least inclined to execute this mandate; the more we reiterated our orders, the more seriously they wagged their turbaned heads, and the more they seemed glued to their respective seats on the elephants. At last the veteran Seesoo, who was my special henchman, raised his voice, and thus expressed the sense of the company. 'O my lords, I am indeed the slave of your highnesses, and were the creature now before us only a tiger, bear, or indeed any four-footed beast, I would at once advance to the combat; but this is an awful brute, and the most baleful of all the inhabitants of this jungle. What can poor people like us do? If any one goes within reach of his long tail, he will be killed to a certainty.'

In short, it was evident that our native friends meant to keep clear of the huge reptile, which they probably mistook for a god, or a devil doing penance on earth, and therefore on no account to be interfered with. So, as my friend assured me that these snakes were not dangerous, I descended from the elephant, and proceeded against it with a heavy hunting-knife. I confess I had some misgivings as to whether his or the natives' estimate of this beast's character might prove correct. It seemed, to say the least, unlikely that nature should entirely deprive the animal of all means of defence for an indefinite time after feeding. What more likely than that it should be able to throw a fold of its body round any one approaching within range? for behind the inflated portion containing the deer there must have been about thirteen feet of the snake in its normal state, and seemingly free to act according to the will of the animal. Any one who has seen a serpent seize a rabbit or a hare will have remarked how the whole body can be used to enfold the prey. Should a limb of the victim protrude, a fold or loop is instantly thrown over it, so that it may be at once compressed with the rest of the body. Bearing all this in mind, I advanced, knife in hand, on a line leading straight to the head of the reptile, and watched narrowly for any sign of its moving; but it remained motionless as I stood over it and looked upon its weird countenance, capable of but one fixed and rigid expression. All its life seemed concentrated in the round bright yellow eyes that returned my gaze with a glittering stare of either rage or fear. I raised the heavy knife, and brought it down with all my might on its neck, thinking to cut its head off. But the bones were solid, and nothing but a horrible gash was the result. Even at this not a muscle stirred, and the eyes glittered and looked piercing as before; the creature seemed entirely without feeling. I was now advised to try and despatch him by severing the spine just behind the great enlargement caused by the body of the parah. I did so; and it instantly lashed out vigorously with the long tail-like end of its body, so that I thought it more prudent to return to its head, and with a few more blows I killed it. We had a measuring-tape in the howdah, by means of which we ascertained that the creature's length was just seventeen feet.

As the brute lay dead at my feet, it struck me that the poor parah stag might still have some life left in it, so with the assistance of some of the natives I extricated it from the serpent's stomach. On its reappearance in the light of day it looked as if it had been neatly trussed for the table. It was about the size of an ordinary sheep, and its head, neck, and limbs were packed into a sort of square, with none of the bones broken, nor were there any signs of external damage. Though an adult stag, it had no horns, as, owing to the time of year, it had shed them. The poor thing, however, was quite dead, and we finally abandoned the two bodies to the tender mercies of the vultures and jackals.

We afterwards regretted that we had not taken the skins of both these animals, and presented them to some museum or clever naturalist, who could, under our superintendence, have represented the snake exactly as we had seen it, lying gorged in front of the rushes. But hunting a tiger under the burning rays of a May sun is enough to occupy all one's thoughts for the time being. As it happened, we might well have spared the time for preparing these specimens, for we were unable to find the tiger, and had to return to our tents empty-handed.

The next day we were more fortunate. Acting on information that we had received, we visited a small patch of dense cane and reeds, not more than twenty or thirty yards in width, and about fifty yards in length. This piece of cover was extremely dense, and so stiff as to appear almost like a solid wall. Four tigers were said to have made this their stronghold, and that in it they invariably spent the long hot hours of the day. At one corner, and touching the edge of the cover, lay the dead body of a cow, over which, through some chink in the herbage, one or more of these animals was probably keeping watch till night and a renewed appetite should come to enable them to finish the banquet which they had only begun by devouring the more succulent parts. But all this was only surmise. There was no sound or movement of any kind to betray the near neighbourhood of a whole family of tigers. The elephants, standing all together, and on an open piece of ground, felt too secure to think it worth while to give any of their usual warnings. Still, there lay the slaughtered cow, and no vultures had ventured to approach it, which showed that they, at any rate, felt sure of the presence of some beast who would pounce on them with lightning speed and unerring aim should they venture to settle upon the carcase.

Whilst we were thus taking an interest in the signs by which we might form some idea of what sport we might expect, men were being sent up trees, and all the usual preparations were made previous to commencing the beat. When all was ready, and the seven elephants were placed in line at one end of the narrow strip, a sudden change came over the manner and bearing of some of these animals. They had doubtless known from the first what was inside this thick bit of cover. Perhaps they thought that by assuming an air of nonchalance we should pass on unsuspiciously to other jungles, and that they would thus get off the danger of beating this nasty-looking place. However that may have been, they were no sooner invited to enter the cane-brake than they all seemed to wake up, and one, called Belculli, positively refused to enter, wheeling round and round, and loudly trumpeting her remonstrances. Her mutiny, however, met with no encouragement from the others. There they all stood, ready to advance. Perhaps, after all, it was better for her to be in the midst of her friends than to run away alone, with the mahout tearing up her wretched head with his sharp and heavy iron goad, as he had begun vigorously to do on the first sign of refractoriness. With some such thoughts as these, she rushed into her place in the rank, and at once commenced to beat with extraordinary energy. Head, shoulders, trunk, all swayed in regular strokes as she cleared the way in front of her. The strip being so narrow, the seven elephants had thorough command of it, and the tigers must have felt what the lark feels when the reaping-machine is bearing down upon her nest, namely that it is time to flit; and before we had got half-way through the cover, the excited cries of our scouts announced that the interesting family had started in different directions in search of more quiet quarters. We followed as fast as we could in the direction that one had been seen to take, and were not long in coming up with it lurking in some scanty bushes, apparently with a view to returning to the cane-brake as soon as we should have left it. This tigress seemed not to have much idea of flight, and she was soon to be seen crouching almost in the open as the elephants advanced upon her. When at about thirty yards from us, she charged, and was shot by my companion from the howdah, without having an opportunity of making any fight.

As soon as we had despatched this animal, we continued our search for the others. My friend caught a sight of one, and fired at it among some watercourses, but with what result was not known at the time, as we could not find it either dead or alive that day. But some distance farther on, where a sort of amphitheatre was formed by a high and perpendicular sandbank making a sort of semicircle, with a deep sunk stream for its base, we suddenly came upon a tiger, who at once charged among the elephants. I fired as it got close under me, when my gun, owing to a bad cartridge, missed fire. My friend, however, hit the brute as it disappeared at great speed. For some time we were unable to find it. At last I got my elephant across to the other side of the stream, and then began inspecting the steep bank. I was not long in seeing the tiger concealing itself among some bushes that grew on the steep slope. I fired at him, and he dropped dead into the stream below. It was not an easy job to haul him out of the water, but it was done at last, and we returned home well pleased with our day's sport, and firmly resolved to drink our own healths in well-cooled champagne, a plentiful supply of which was carried for us by our camels.

CHAPTER XI.

WE decided to remain in this neighbourhood for a day or two longer to hunt the remaining two tigers that had been turned out of the cane-brake. We thought that even though they might not return to the exact spot where we had first found them, that still they would probably not move more than a mile or so in search of fresh quarters. And sure enough the morning but one after bagging the two first tigers, my friend came upon the dead body of the one he had fired at just before sighting the second of those we had killed, and which he naturally supposed was the same one making off. It was lying exposed to view close to where he had fired at it, but having its skin on, no feathered or four-footed scavengers had ventured to approach it. Having been dead nearly forty-eight hours, of course it was in too decomposed a state to admit of being skinned. It is very annoying to think of how many animals which one is supposed to have missed altogether, must in the course of events be really lying dead within a hundred yards of one. In a temperate climate the hunter would, of course, always have a few dogs to track the wounded beast. But in the jungles of India, the sun, even during most of the 'cold weather,' is too hot to admit of hounds being out all day.

We might perhaps have met with the fourth tiger, but time

was now an object, and we were obliged to direct our steps to a place called Jalabund, so as to enable my friend to visit the headquarters of his business, which was contiguous to this village. During his absence I used to beat the large bojee, which was close at hand, but without ever even seeing any large animal. One afternoon on returning from one of these unsuccessful beats to my tent, which was pitched under some large trees, an amusing circumstance occurred. I had hardly dismounted from my elephant, and taken a look round, when I saw an excited mob issuing from the gates of the village that occupied some rising ground about a hundred yards off. At the head of the noisy throng I recognized my own major-domo—a Portuguese, or I should say a Goanese Christian—gesticulating wildly, and doubtless doing his best to get his voice above the others. This, however, must have been quite impossible, for the din made by fifty or sixty natives, all screaming their loudest, was such as to drown any single performer. As they approached me, the emulation of each waxed in intensity, till at last they all halted in front of me like a crew of raging maniacs. To make myself heard was quite out of the question, and my signs, imploring or commanding silence, only seemed to add fuel to the flames. Under ordinary circumstances, I should have charged amongst them with a stick, but this might have led to complications, and been a source of annoyance to my friend on his return the next day. I looked around for an inspiration, and my eye fell on a little writing table neatly set out with pens, ink, and various kinds of paper. I seized this and placed it in front of the infuriated crowd, took a chair, seated myself, and, pen in hand, spread out an imposing clean sheet of foolscap. By this time I had observed a young man whom the others seemed to regard as a leader. On him I fixed my eyes intently, and then pretended to write down whatever came from his mouth.

'Good gracious,' he thought, 'this must be an expert Government reporter.' And in an instant he was as one struck dumb; not another word would he utter. The rest of the mob were even more cowed, and a dead silence now succeeded to the late frantic clamour. I looked judicially around, and said: 'Well, go on.' But no one would go on; all looked towards the earth, except the brave young chief, who stared, panic-stricken, across the crowd at a white-bearded old gentleman, his father, and chief *en titre* of the settlement, but whose authority had been usurped by his son. These two worthies having looked hard at one another for some moments, the younger one exclaimed, 'We are guilty.'

'Certainly,' I said; 'of course you are,'—though I knew not of what; so I thought it best to continue thus,—'I shall not, however, try you here, but remove you to-morrow on the elephants to Palanpore, where there is a regular court. See that you are all ready by break of day.' With this I dismissed them.

As I expected, a deputation waited on me a few hours after, to say that matters had been satisfactorily arranged with my butler, and that they hoped the idea of a trial might be abandoned. To this I need hardly say I graciously assented, as it was exactly the turn I had been manœuvring for, and by reason of which all was smooth and peaceful when my kind friend and guide rejoined me. This he did the next day, and we once more started on our wanderings.

At the next halting-ground we met with a sporting engineer, who spent the day with us. He informed me that in this very district the swamps were so deep and treacherous that when out on one occasion with a large party he had seen an elephant sink at once out of sight, leaving his mahout seated on the soft surface. The driver must have had his feet free of the elephant's neck-band, or kelāwar, in which they usually stick their feet, or he would have shared the poor brute's fate. It sank so deep that no trace of its body could be felt, even with the aid of long bamboos, which were thrust into the bog to try and discover where it might be lying. I asked if the elephant had had time to utter any cry, and my informant answered, 'Yes, it gave one pitiful little squeak.' The truth of this story can be vouched for by many others besides the gentleman that told it to me, and whose authority alone is quite sufficient to establish the fact as far as I am concerned.

I had now, alas! arrived near the end of my very pleasant trip through the Terai. We were to have a final beat at a place called Kelody, but without much prospect of success, as the natives only gave vague accounts of a tigress that was supposed to be in the vicinity. However, the jungle was as good as any we had seen, so there was no cause to despair.

After beating for some time, we found ourselves advancing along some streams, bounded by a bank on one side of perhaps fifty feet in height, whilst the opposite shore was quite flat, and merged into never-ending plains and woods. Of course there was the usual amount of profuse vegetation in all directions, whilst just under the cliff-like bank there were frequent beds of high and dense rushes. My friend, on the howdah elephant, steered along the top of this high bank, whilst I kept the other end of the line, out on the plain. Each mahout carried a policeman's rattle, which I had brought with me from England, and had served out to them at the beginning of the trip. As one of the elephants was passing through a bed of rushes, it came to a dead stop, and the mahout called out that there must be something in front of him. At the same moment the rushes began to move in such a way that I at once called out that there was a tiger in this lair. I ordered the mahout, who was close to the animal, to halt till we could all join him, and we were not long before we got all abreast. I then gave the word to advance with all the rattles in full swing. This was no doubt the right line of conduct, for we soon heard a great rush, followed by the report of my friend's rifle. We hurried on to learn the result, when I suddenly saw a large tigress flying back towards me, and well exposed to view as she dashed across a wide and shallow sheet of water. I gave her another bullet, and she fell, if I remember rightly, at once, to rise no more. We loaded her on an elephant, and took her to our tents to be skinned as usual.

For some reason or other, the inhabitants of this large village were unusually anxious to obtain the flesh of the brute to eat, and we could have no objection to their taking it. They carried it all away piecemeal, but naturally I kept the four young male cubs that would have been born in another day or two at the latest. Though quite perfect, they had never breathed, and were in size somewhere between a rabbit and a rat. No doubt it was unfortunate that this tigress should have been killed when just about to add four fine young tigers to the population; but I see no means of avoiding such catastrophes, for I do not think there is any special breeding time for these animals, and besides, in theory at least, their total extermination is to be compassed if possible.

We now commenced our homeward march, beating, of course, as we went. The country gradually changed its character as we neared the borders of the Terai. Sand, gravel, and even stones began to appear. There were also wide dry beds of nullahs, which pursued their winding way through a land more resembling the ordinary plains of Central India than anything to be seen in the districts we had just left. It was in one of these broad shallow beds, which are dry at this time of the year, that a panther was known to lurk. Our search proved fruitless, so we all assembled in the middle of the nullah, on our elephants, and began to discuss the advisability of retiring from the scene, when suddenly there was a great commotion, and my mahout, behind whom I was sitting, suddenly set to with all his might at Muaruk Guj's head, so as to cause him to make all speed towards the bank. I looked round and saw all the rest of the mahouts doing the same, except one. Whilst we had been standing talking quite composedly on this apparently hard and stony bottom, the great weight of the elephants had been telling gradually on what was in reality only a hard-baked upper crust. This had suddenly given way under the feet of poor Bijli, and she found herself immersed in a quicksand that reached quite up to the pad on which her driver was sitting. No doubt in a few moments more all the other elephants would have been in the same plight. As it was, however, they gained the bank in safety, where they were eventually joined by their unlucky companion, who had succeeded in extricating herself, but only after a long and painful struggle, during which she had suffered an agony of fright. On such occasions it is seldom that anything can be done to assist the unfortunate beast. Such ropes as one has are neither long nor stout enough to be of any use, and the same may be said of the insignificant quantity of brushwood that a small party of five or six men could collect and throw to the animal to make a roadway for itself.

This was the last little mishap that we met with before our return to Ramnugger, where the party was to break up. On arriving here, preparations were at once made for a general cleaning and feasting. Sheep were presented to our followers, and the elephants were treated to great blocks of 'goor,' which is brown sugar in one of its earliest stages. As Bijli raised her trunk, and opened her queer-looking mouth in expectation of the usual donation of a few pieces the size of one's fist, I carefully adjusted between her back teeth a lump larger than a man's head. I shall never forget the expression of her little eyes as she received this *bonne bouche.* She kept her head raised aloft to prevent the juice from running out, and then directed her eyes down on me, beaming with elephantine pleasure. She could not swallow the prize; it was too big. Nor could she divide it; it was too sticky. All she could do was to hold it tight, and roll her eyes, till it melted. These were doubtless the happiest moments of her life.

The last thing I did was to assist at a great bathing of the elephants. The deep pool where I had shot the mahseer was selected for this pleasant performance. The water was so beautifully clear that one could see the whole form of these huge creatures as they swam underneath, with only the mahouts and a portion of their trunks above the surface. Being myself in bathing costume, I mounted the neck of Muaruk Guj, and invited him to slide in. But instead of doing so he sat down on the brink, and waved his trunk about, beseeching to be let off. I was then told that this elephant was not accustomed to swimming, and could not be taught by making him slide at once out of his depth. He preferred lying on his side and having his back scrubbed with jagged stones by his attendants. I therefore mounted another elephant who was accustomed to this amusement, and was soon disporting myself with the rest. Unfortunately, I found as soon as the performance was over, and I had cooled down, that I had contrived to sprain my leg so severely that riding was out of the question for some time to come. I had, therefore, on taking leave of the friend who had so kindly enabled me to see all this sport in the Terai, and whose headquarters were at Ramnugger, to travel reclining on the pad of an elephant till I reached the travellers' bungalow at Kaladoonghi, a distance of sixteen or eighteen miles. It is from this bungalow that one can start, on a well-made road, either back to the distant railway station at Moradabad, or one can ascend the mountains, and after a journey of about sixteen miles, arrive at the beautiful hill station of Nynee Tāl. As I had still about ten days of unexpired leave, I resolved to go and spend three days with some very nice friends that I had at this place, and who had kindly invited me to go and see them in their lovely mountain home. The road the whole way up the mountain is broad and beautifully kept, but, owing to its steepness and many curves, no great pace can be achieved, and it took me five or six hours to accomplish the journey. A contrivance known as a jompon is the most pleasant vehicle in which to traverse these roads. It is a chair which varies in size and shape, and is supported on long poles borne on the shoulders of men called 'jompon wallas.' For all expeditions beyond the mere limits of the station, not less than sixteen of these men are employed with each chair, who relieve each other in sets of eight.

Thus comfortably seated, 'facing the horses,' if I may be allowed the expression, the traveller smoothly ascends the seven thousand feet by which Nynee Tāl overtops the sea. The way lies through beautifully-wooded mountain slopes. Magnificent forests of giant pines replace the spongy jungles of the Terai, whilst the air as you rise becomes every moment more and more rarified and exhilarating, till one soon ceases to wonder that beings who have been trained through many generations to luxuriate in the swamps below, find a difficulty in existing in this highly-favoured region.

When you have surmounted the last of the many ups and downs of which the road is composed, and turned the corner formed by the jutting rocks that bristle down the crest of the final spur of the overhanging mountains, Nynee Tāl strikes the eye of the expectant traveller like a vision of fairyland. It consists of a vast amphitheatre, the centre of which is occupied by a large and deep lake of clear water, in which are beautifully reflected the mighty mountains that rise abruptly all round its margin. Also the thousand glittering and beautiful abodes of pleasure that everywhere and at all altitudes peep from the masses of dark foliage, or stand out boldly on some projecting crag, are all faithfully depicted in the same beautiful mirror. A well-made road runs round the lake, at one end of which has been built the bazaar, containing many good shops. There is also space to be found for lawn-tennis grounds, and other places of public amusement. No business is done in this happy valley. It has, from the time of its first occupancy by the English, been devoted exclusively to holiday-making by such as feel that they can bear the sultry heat of the plains no longer. The place having from its very birth been devoted to pleasure, happiness, and luxury, naturally always wears a gala aspect, and is, in fact, continually *en fête*. Alas! that the innocent and joyous lives of the inhabitants should occasionally be overwhelmed with wild and terrific confusion. Times occasionally come when the side of a mountain may suddenly be seen sliding down into the lake. The pretty villas fall, and are engulphed with as much ease as though they were built of cards. Terrible then is the scene of woe and desolation. Women and children, lately full of life and hope, are dug out from the ruins—mangled corpses; scarce to be recognized by their heart-broken friends. But let us not dwell on so sad a picture, which is, after all, only to be seen once in a lifetime. Many are the happy months spent annually at this delightful sanitarium by hundreds of our countrymen and countrywomen, who, but for some such place of refuge from the frightful heat of the plains, would certainly succumb to their ailments, and leave their bones in a foreign land. Few, if any people, take their carriages to this settlement, as they could only be used upon the road immediately surrounding the lake. The cautious and prudent either walk or are carried in jompons, whilst the more venturesome mount horses or ponies, which should be accustomed to these mountains, or they will be not unlikely to shy over the numerous precipices with which the place abounds. It is a pity that this portion of the Himalayas has no near peaks covered with eternal snow. One such, with its reflection in the lake, would add immensely to the effect of the landscape. My hostess, however, was kind enough to go with me on horseback to a spot where a turn of the path opened on an extensive view of, I believe, thirty or forty miles. Here a seat had been erected, and was known as the 'snow seat,' because from it you could see the mountains rolling away from you in successive and ever-heightening ranges, till at last the prospect was closed by a dim white line, which was the far-off snowy range. What mysterious heights and depths, what awful ravines lay between us and those untrodden regions! Only the eagle might explore them safely. But if the lake could reflect no hoary and celebrated mountain, it was not without its points of romantic interest. One high black rock springs from its bosom, and overhangs the water at a height of about fifty feet. The summit can be gained from the land side; and it is asserted by the oldest inhabitants that a lover once threw himself from this eminence on being challenged by his 'ladye fair' to do something, no matter what, to show that he really loved her!

The story then goes on to relate, how the young man determined to take the proud beauty at her word, and that so suddenly and unexpectedly, that she should have no time to retract or explain away her promise. This she might have done, had he set out into the jungle to beard the tiger in his den, or to climb the dizzy precipices in pursuit of the Himalayan chamois. Such feats would require some time to prepare for, and still more to carry into execution. And, worse than all, he would have to go away—quite away! What might not occur during his absence, and before he had had time to perform any deed, such as he could hope would gain the approval of his mistress? He might return loaded, it is true, with honour and glory, but only to find his idol wedded to a hated rival! No, no! something must be done on the spot, and at once!

Thus he ruminated as he sat with a faithful friend, on a rustic seat overlooking the lake. As his eye wandered listlessly over the scenery, searching vainly for an inspiring thought, it fell upon the great black rock, which suddenly seemed to start into life, and to advise him to spring from its overhanging apex into the water below. Yes, this should be the 'something' that he would do!

'Come,' he said calmly to his friend, 'let us ascend yon cliff.'

To this proposal his unsuspecting companion at once assented, and with some difficulty they reached the dangerous goal. Then without an instant's warning, and with a wild cry, that sounded like the name of his beloved, he sprang from the giddy height, and fell with an ominous splash into the lake below.

How he was rescued from the watery depths I could

not exactly learn, but it would appear that, but for the timely help of his friend, his life would have ended at this tragic moment.

Doubtless, to an experienced diver a plunge of fifty feet would be a very small matter, but our hero was not trained to such evolutions in the air, and therefore fell upon the surface of the water with such a crash, that it was doubtful for some time whether life could be restored to his inanimate frame. Consciousness, however, returned in a short time, so he was carried home and prosaically put to bed.

We may be sure it was not long before the thoughtless maiden was apprised of the deeds of her swain, and of the sad plight to which her cruel words had reduced him. Full of remorse, which was destined soon to turn to love, she flew to the side of his couch, where her tender ministrations were most efficacious in restoring health to the sufferer. He soon entirely recovered, led the lady of his choice to the hymeneal altar, and lived happily ever after.

Such, reader, is the tradition of the 'Lover's Rock' as it was told to me, and the truth of which I have no reason to doubt. But, of course, I can only answer positively for such things as I have either seen or done myself.

By the time my short stay at Nynee Tāl came to an end, I had sufficiently recovered from the sprain I had received, whilst bathing on the neck of the elephant, to be able to face a terribly hot journey to less favoured regions, without any more discomfort than was inevitable under the circumstances.

On arriving at Moradabad I found myself at no great distance from Rampore, where the rajah lived who had so kindly lent us the elephants. I therefore hired a stagecoach, and caused myself to be driven to his capital that I might personally thank him for the pleasure his generosity had afforded me. Unfortunately, on arriving at my destination, I was informed that his highness was too ill to see me, so I had to drive back again without obtaining an interview with the only sovereign that ever did me a personal service.

Thus terminated my shooting trip in the Terai, and with it as happy a two months as I ever remember to have spent in my life.

CHAPTER XII.

SUCH is the effect of steam, that after travelling for the brief space of four days, I found myself in a land so distant from my late happy hunting grounds, and differing so much from them in every respect, that I asked myself sadly, 'Can there be such a place as the Terai? Those matchless jungles in which I have so lately roamed, are they but a splendid dream?'

I was bound for Baroda, the capital of Goozerat, and at this place I duly arrived, after tarrying sufficiently long at Mhow to enable me to settle my affairs at that place, and make one of those fresh starts for a new station, to which every old Indian has to get accustomed.

The whole climate from Cape Comorin to the Himalayas is bad, or at any rate trying, to persons of unmixed European descent. It might therefore seem to the reader that no move could be worse than the oft-quoted one of 'from the frying-pan into the fire.' But this is very far from being the case. In India, or I might say Asia, endless phrases of suffering can be found, the mildest of which fully justifies the high salaries that are paid to all who exile themselves to those tropical regions. Certainly the pay is good, and as high as the taxpayers can afford to make it. The sport is also on such a grand scale, that it enables those who have a taste for it to enjoy life so thoroughly that all the drawbacks and disagreeables are forgotten.

Still, there are moments when one's philosophy is severely tried, as, for instance, when one receives an order to quit Mhow, and hasten to any place in the province of Goozerat, just in time for the commencement of the monsoon, as the rainy season is called.

This was exactly my case. I must go; there was no escape from the dismal swamp, fit only at this time of the year for frogs, and such other reptiles as are born of malaria. The natives themselves suffer fearfully from fever, with occasional outbursts of cholera, and other, such as may be called first-class diseases. I was thankful that, not being a native, nor chained like them by family ties to the spot, I could cast about for some means of escape. In spite, however, of my best efforts, I remained a whole month at this place.

Never shall I forget the horrible soppy moisture of this particular climate. I am sure I perspired in that one month as much as an ordinary inhabitant of the British Isles does in a whole lifetime. Owing to the constant and heavy 'downpours' of rain, the country in all directions was more or less under water, and all excursions into the jungle were stopped as a matter of course.

To pass the time, we depended on such amusements as the camp and neighbouring city might afford. The Guicowar, as the native ruler of this state is called, was rich, and it so happened that at this time a number of entertainments were being given in honour of the little boy who had just succeeded by adoption to the throne in place of his predecessor, who had been deposed by the English Government. The nautches and the dinners I did not care for, but I was very glad to witness for once one of the great displays in the arena, of which the Guicowar and all his subjects are so fond, that the supreme Government has not, as yet, had the heart to put a stop to the sports therein enacted, and which are stigmatized by the more sensitive of our countrymen as brutalizing and degrading.

Without entering into the merits of the question, I must own that I took sufficient interest in the proceedings to feel a wish to describe them. The arena is very spacious and, of course, without a roof. A gallery overlooking it can be entered from the palace, and it is divided into two compartments, one for the accommodation of the English and higher classes of natives, and the other is devoted to the ladies of the palace, who can see everything, and only be seen as much as may be warranted by their rank, age, and other considerations. Over this gallery there is a roof that effectually keeps off the rays of the sun. And really, as I sat in this well-shaded retreat at four in the afternoon, when the great heat of the day was over, and in the company of many friends surveyed the exciting scenes below, I could not wonder at the strong partiality of the people for this their favourite spectacle. All round the sides of this sort of circus they formed a great crowd of spectators, who could admire everything, including the combats of wild beasts, in perfect safety, owing to the height of the barricades, above which their seats or standing ground rose in tiers.

First came the wrestlers, whose training and performances are so different to anything one would see of the same kind in Europe. They seem to rely more on weight than wind, for they are undeniably fat, very fat. The muscles do not seem to stand out at all from the surface of the skin, nor do they show any of those signs of 'condition' which are looked for in a northern athlete. Two champions having stepped from among their fellows into a clear space, they at once assume a semi-sitting posture, and fix their eyes ferociously on one another. In this position they begin to describe semicircles round about each other, getting nearer the while, and making loud claps by striking their hollow palms on their own plump limbs. This and other manœuvres continue for a tediously long time, and are no doubt intended by each combatant to distract the attention of the other; always, however, as far as I could see, without success, as they invariably ended by glaring into one another's faces, quite immoveable, in the same stooping attitude, and their noses almost touching. Such being the result, I have always wondered why they did not begin at this point, at which indeed the real business seems to commence. They now make lightning snatches at one another to get a favourable hold, and I must say they parry one another's attacks in this respect with wonderful adroitness. This skirmishing, however, cannot go on for ever, and at last the combatants are locked in that embrace which is to give victory to one, and generally an honourable defeat to the other. Sometimes the umpires have to declare a drawn battle, but this is not often the case.

In turn with the wrestlers the swordsmen show their skill. These men usually perform with stout sticks, encased in thick leather, which I believe does not quite touch the stick;

so that though this weapon can deal very painful blows, no bones are likely to be broken by its instrumentality. Each of these 'swords' has a strong hilt to protect the hand, and the performer has a small round shield of stout hide about the size of a dinner plate, which he bears on the knuckles of his left fist, with which to intercept the blows of his assailant.

Like the wrestlers, the sword-players adopt a crouching and springing motion, much of which is no doubt done for effect. Between the different assaults they circle round one another with abundant flourishing and gesticulation. In this way the combat proceeds till the umpires decide which is the best man, or till they think it is time to allow another couple to show their skill.

Before the spectators have had time to weary of these interesting sports all the performers vanish, and at a given signal the owners of the fighting rams group themselves in the foreground, each in charge of his own woolly favourite. The matches have all been told off beforehand, so that in the course of half an hour many pairs of these handsome and spirited little beasts have been shown off. With their well-cleaned, curly coats, bright eyes, and twisted horns, they are well worth looking at as each stands straining to escape from its master's hold, in order to encounter its enemy. Both are liberated at the same instant, and bound with extraordinary velocity at one another, so that their heads meet with what one would suppose to be a crushing blow. Neither, however, seems any the worse, and they retire of their own accords a yard or so, and repeat the same feat. This they do as often as their owners think fit to allow, and when at last they are separated, they trot off with great contentment, and have evidently enjoyed the *séance* quite as much as the lookers-on. The truth is, that these people are very fond of their respective animals, and never allow them to fight *à outrance;* so that it is only when an unforeseen accident occurs, such as I shall have to detail before the end of this chapter, that any of these dumb performers suffer at all, or that there is anything like cruelty to complain of. At least such has been my experience of these meetings.

To the rams succeeded the contending buffaloes. These beasts, I was told, seldom display much spirit for the fray, and are in consequence generally reckoned 'slow.' I was therefore quite unprepared for the sight that was in store for me when the first pair of bulls were ushered in from opposite doors of the arena. Both were certainly magnificent specimens of their race. They seemed to have been trained on the same principles as the human gladiators, for as each stood surrounded by a little posse of his attendants that prevented him from at once seeing his rival, one could observe that their smooth and almost hairless black skins shone with an oily lustre on their rounded and well-filled carcases. Each animal was about the size of a large English bull, but of more massive structure, especially about the head and horns, which were in these specimens of enormous thickness at the roots, whence they took a sudden curve and terminated in a total length of not more than twenty-four or thirty inches. They were symmetrically placed upon their colossal foreheads, and presented a much more workmanlike appearance than the long thin horns that usually adorn these beasts, and which I once saw reach back to the animal's tail.

The two buffaloes now under review were soon got into a

position fairly facing one another. Each was tossing its head, rolling its glaring eyes, and sniffing the impending combat with dilated nostrils, when each group of half-naked attendants stepped back and disclosed them to one another's view. For an instant they seemed transfixed with rage, and then appeared literally to fly through the air as though their huge heavy bodies had been propelled by some gigantic catapult. They met front to front in mid-air with an astounding crash, such as caused them to shiver from their horns to the tips of their long extended tails.

If I had not seen it, I would not have believed that anything of flesh and blood could have stood so tremendous a shock. For a moment each combatant stood paralyzed, and apparently in expectation that his opponent really would fall down dead. But, as this was evidently the last thing that either of them intended to do, they speedily pulled themselves together, and renewed the struggle with unabated spirit, though, as they were now at close quarters, with much diminished effect.

Long before either animal had really begun to tire of the tournament, the signal was given to separate them. Then it was amusing to see how these powerful and highly-infuriated creatures seemed to recognize and respect their human friends and companions; how they submitted to have their tails tugged at by unclad urchins, whilst others ran at the sides of their heads with nothing but walking-sticks, endeavouring to explain to them that they must go different ways. These measures were not attended with immediate success, as the bulls were by no means inclined to discontinue the struggle for the mastery. They seemed, however, equally determined not to injure their well-known allies, and ended by getting into such a state of general bewilderment that each evidently thought he had better make off for his accustomed stable, in the quiet retirement of which he might revolve a fresh plan of attack for the next occasion.

As soon as the arena was cleared, other pairs of buffaloes were introduced in the same manner as the first. But their behaviour was generally marked by inefficiency and tameness. Some altogether falsified the proud boasts of their masters, and refused to make even a show of fighting. These were hustled ignominiously from the scene—doubtless to appear again with much the same result another time.

Indeed, during this *fête* there was only one other pair of these beasts besides those I have already described that seemed inclined to tackle one another. These had both very long attenuated horns sloping back towards their hind quarters. Their general appearance, too, was not equal to that of the first pair. However, on being driven up to one another, the more spirited of the two made a charge, which was duly met by his antagonist. A good deal of pushing and battling now ensued, in the midst of which the one who was least able to give the other any advantage got his front foot over his own long unwieldy horn, and could not get it back again; he had accomplished the feat of getting himself completely into chancery. Of course the poor thing fell at once, and was immediately set upon by his relentless adversary, who pommelled his fallen foe with bloodthirsty eagerness. Fortunately the victor's horns were ill-shaped and blunt, or he would at once have mortally wounded the wretched victim which lay moaning on the ground.

As soon as the attendants had realized the nature of the catastrophe, they ran for a rope, affixed it to the hind leg of the oppressor, and would quickly have hauled him off, only that the rope, which was an absurdly thin one, snapped, and another and stouter one had to be procured. With this the excited beast was dragged away, and the wounded one, having had its leg liberated, was able to walk from the arena, but with one wound, at least, which I should think must have rendered its recovery doubtful. Thus terminated the part played by the buffaloes in this entertainment, and which were productive of the only *contretemps* that occurred throughout the proceedings.

The pageant was brought to a close by a contest between two large male rhinoceroses. At first these creatures seemed so apathetic that it looked as if nothing was to come of their interview; but by dint of a little persuasion they were induced to attack one another. There was nothing brilliant in their movements, but plenty of determination was manifested.

With his pointed upper lip ever on the ground, each drove his long upright horn before him as though he were engaged in ploughing; at least this is what he would have done had not his opponent carefully kept his nose touching that of his adversary, whose advance thus became impossible. They were well matched, and if one was made to recede a little he speedily recovered his ground. Each evidently felt that it would be fatal to let the other get under his guard. This, no doubt, sooner or later, would have occurred; but I suppose it was not intended that either of these valuable animals should be sacrificed, so, after they had been allowed to display their curious method of attack and defence for about a quarter of an hour, they were separated, and removed to their private quarters. This operation was not so simple as it had been in the case of the buffaloes. It was easy to see that the rhinoceroses would have had no objection to slaughter any number of the human race without respect to persons; but they had doubtless often performed ere this, and were aware that it would be useless to try and catch any of their nimble keepers. They therefore retired without very much ado.

Thus terminated the only spectacle of this kind that I had ever witnessed. The programme on such occasions is never twice the same; sometimes elephants are made to contend, and I have even heard of a tiger being turned out to fight with a buffalo. In this case, I believe, the tiger was killed, which is not surprising, as it had doubtless been brought up from infancy a captive in a small cage, and could have no experience in the art of self-defence.

As I shall probably not again refer to native sports and pastimes, I will conclude the subject by giving an account of a really wonderful performance that I once saw executed with a sharp sword.

At the station of Mhow, about the time of which I am writing, weekly games were held by the native regiments there, and in connection with these I had heard, before my arrival at that place, of a havildar, *i.e.* sergeant, of one of the corps doing duty there, who regularly every week performed the most extraordinary feats in the presence of a large assembly of spectators.

Availing myself of the first opportunity that occurred after my arrival, I attended the meeting, which was held one

Thursday afternoon in the open air. After the usual wrestling, tumbling, and sword-play had been gone through, the space was cleared, and the man in whom the chief interest was centred stood before his judges. He was a fine-looking fellow in the prime of life, and notwithstanding the frightfully critical nature of what he was going to do, he moved about with perfect ease and calmness. In one hand he held a very long double-edged sword, sharp at the point, and with edges like razors. With the other hand he led his little son, a child aged about six years, who was also clearly well accustomed to what was to follow. From the little fellow's evident enjoyment of the scene, it was plain that failure on the part of his father was a thing quite beyond the limits of his imagination.

As soon as the usual preliminary ceremonies had been gone through, such as walking round and salaaming to the commanding officer and principal guests, the father placed his little boy in the centre of the circle, with a small lime (a kind of lemon) about twice the size of a walnut under his heel. Then, taking up his stand a few feet from the child, he grasped firmly the hilt of the sword, and began brandishing the weapon rapidly in the air. The blade was thin and finely tempered, so that it could be seen to quiver and undulate throughout its entire length as it flashed in the rays of the setting sun. Suddenly the muscles of the athlete might be seen to stiffen themselves; an instant's pause, then a sudden and lightning-like swoop, and the lime under the boy's heel was safely severed.

Such of my readers as are familiar with India will think nothing of the feat above detailed, and will exclaim, 'Oh, this is nothing; we have seen this done at every meeting of native swordsmen.' Thus they will bear witness to the wonderful correctness of eye and firmness of nerve possessed by these men. But I do not think many, even of the oldest inhabitants of the East, have often witnessed a performance equal to that with which this havildar was wont to conclude his exhibition.

The boy having taken up his position as before, a small open box, about the size of those we use for tooth-powder, was placed on the ground at his feet. It was filled with a black powder called soorma, used by the natives for darkening the eyelashes. Round this little box, and about the boy's head, the sword was now made to play with redoubled velocity. In the midst of the most dazzling passes the weapon would dart towards the little box, and then reappear, steadily poised at the full stretch of the performer's arm, in front of the eyes of the child; then a sudden turn of the wrist, and a heavy dark line of powder was lying on one of the boy's lower eyelashes, placed there by the sharp point of the long sword. The same was then done to the other eye. This feat was performed weekly, always with undeviating success, and was certainly the most wonderful instance of nerve and steadiness that I ever witnessed.

CHAPTER XIII.

I WAS not long at Baroda after witnessing the sports which I have endeavoured to describe, and was very glad soon to find myself at Poona, the capital of the Deccan, and the largest military station in Western India. Here the climate during the monsoon is so excellent, that it is looked upon as a sanitarium during the rains. The rainfall is moderate, not exceeding forty inches, which, combined as it is with an altitude above the sea of two thousand feet, always ensures a nice fresh air, free from excessive dampness or too much heat.

Immediately on my arrival in the month of July, I began to meditate as to how I should manage to get away into a tiger jungle on the 1st of the next ensuing April, and as to which jungle I had better fix upon. Meanwhile, and long before anything appeared clear to me, I thought there could be no harm in at once making the acquaintance and studying the various characters of the large number of elephants kept at this place by Government; for though I might not require them for this next trip, there was no knowing at what time my knowledge might not be of the utmost use to me. The vast yard, surrounded by a low wall two or three feet high, in which all the mules, horses, camels, elephants, and other Government beasts stand in the open air in many ranks, may be entered by any one who cares to go and take an inspection. And in addition to this, I was shortly placed in the commissariat, which gave me, in a measure, charge of all the live stock. Under such favourable circumstances, I was speedily in possession of all that I cared to know of the elephants.

The females I tabooed *en masse*, although there was one who gave signs of a fighting disposition. This amiable creature, when she saw strangers enter the gates, would at once secrete a stone half-way down her throat, and on the unsuspecting visitors approaching within range, she would disinter the missile with her trunk, and hurl it at their luckless heads! She seldom, however, had a chance of exercising her aim, which would not, even with practice, have qualified her for any known class in musketry, as all stones were carefully kept out of her reach. Of the males, some were known to be timid, others so outrageously savage, that as far as I could learn they had ceased to be of any use. Eventually, two splendid tuskers were shown me, whose characters were at all events worthy of discussion. The one I liked best was called Futteh Alli. He was of immense size, and stood ten feet three inches at the shoulder. He was, however, only recommended doubtfully, and with much head-shaking on the part of his mahout, Mahomed Yakoob, who produced from a leather pocket-book a certificate from a certain Colonel H—— to the effect that Futteh Alli was a most dangerous brute, that he and a friend had been hunted by him, and that they would certainly have been killed, but for the courageous efforts of Mahomed Yakoob, who was driving him at the time.

'You see, sahib,' he added, 'this elephant is a beast void of religion (be imān), and he hates the English!'

'Dear me,' I rejoined, 'and how does he get on with the natives?'

'Oh,' he said, 'much better, but still he is uncertain even with them; he has killed two, and there is but little doubt that he will do even for me, his keeper, sooner or later.'

Notwithstanding this unsatisfactory character of the animal, I felt an unaccountable attraction towards him. I never saw an elephant that looked more amiable; he had such lively ways, and would do little tricks at the command of his mahout. I used almost daily to mount the raised dais when he was at home, and put some sugar or bread into his mouth, so that he might come to recognize me. On these occasions Yakoob Khan always seemed very nervous, and used to wedge himself between me and the elephant till I got down from the stand. I was, however, full of misplaced confidence, and was certain I could control the animal better than the keeper himself.

One afternoon I considered myself fortunate in arriving before Futteh Alli when no one was in sight. I drew up in front of him with a few small pieces of chopped sugar-cane in my hand. I looked attentively at the colossus, and could observe no signs of any unusual emotion. I spoke to him in those tones which I flattered myself he considered dulcet. On this he gently waved his ears, and twinkled his eyes, as who should say, 'It is all right; you are my friend.' I now called out cheerfully, 'Salaam, Futteh Alli, salaam!' and raised my arm at the same time. To this he responded by lifting his trunk over his head, to return the salute. This last act made assurance doubly sure. I mounted the platform, and as I did so the elephant again flung up his trunk, and opened his mouth as if to accept with gratitude my sweet and juicy offerings. But his heart was full of treachery. He well knew that with his front feet manacled it would be useless to try and pursue me even if I had but a few inches' start of him. He therefore dissembled with great cleverness and self-command till I had actually leant up against one of his tusks, and had got my hand in his mouth; then he suddenly belched forth a shout of rage, and made a sweep at me with his tusks that sent me flying off the platform into the dust below, whilst my hat was hurled in the other direction. I sat up bareheaded and half-stunned, just in time to see the under-keeper, who had been slumbering behind a heap of equipments all the time, sent with still greater force in a backward direction. He also assumed a sitting posture, and cast such doleful looks at me, that I thought to encourage him by laughing and nodding towards him. The elephant, meanwhile, had thrown off the mask, and it was evidently only the shackles of his front feet that prevented him from getting off his platform and finishing one of us. The poor keeper would have been the victim, for, as I soon saw, he was too much hurt to move, so I had him picked up and sent in a litter to the hospital, where it was discovered that his ribs were broken.

By this time a crowd had gathered in a circle, of which the enraged elephant was the centre. From amongst the excited throng an energetic native now rushed with a long spear in his hand, and began to prod at the elephant as he stood, foot-bound, on his dais. But Futteh Alli was in no mood to submit to the usual discipline of captive elephants; so, no sooner did this zealous keeper point the weapon at him, than he wrenched it from his grasp, put it crosswise in his mouth, and stood at ease, surveying the now gaping assembly. And very imposing he looked in this attitude, but his conduct had no doubt been most reprehensible, and certainly deserved to be punished. I wished him to be flogged by my second favourite, Bundoola, who, though not so tall as Futteh Alli, was a magnificent tusker, and the only thing in the yard of which the delinquent was afraid. There seemed to be no doubt that Bundoola would advance with a chain in his trunk, and give the criminal a good drubbing; but this course was considered too hazardous, as it might lead to much injury of Government property.

Fortunately I was not hurt, as owing to my actually leaning on the elephant's tusk, when he swooped at me, the force of the blow was lost, and I was only tossed in the air. His feet being manacled, he thought he could not trample on me, and these animals are very chary of using their trunks for fighting purposes. Some never do so, as they are instinctively aware that it is by this powerful but delicate organ that they get their living, and that any serious injury to it might cause their death by starvation. With all this animal's intelligence, it had luckily not struck him that with what to him would have been an imperceptible squeeze of this flexible member, all my bones could have been crushed in an instant. Taking, then, everything into consideration, I felt I had got off better than could have been expected, and that I could afford to let the account between myself and Futteh Alli stand open till I had driven him myself against at least one wounded tiger.

With these reflections I resolved to declare a truce, and even to make friends. I advanced, therefore, towards him as he still stood brandishing the broken spear, and again addressed him by name in quite my usual tone of voice. This certainly seemed to take him aback more than any amount of scolding, for he dropped the remains of the spear, and contemplated me with a fixed stare, which might have meant anything. I did not again mount the platform, but stood in front of it just within reach of the animal's trunk. 'Take this, Futteh Alli,' I said, and held out the very same dainty morsel that he had already tasted. He accepted the invitation, put out his proboscis, and took the offering peacefully from my hand. In this way I gave him all that I had brought, and then retired from the scene. It was not, however, deemed safe for any one to go near him for three or four days after this event, so during that time his food and water were conveyed to him from a safe distance by means of simple arrangements familiar to all keepers of elephants.

I would ask my readers kindly to remember these two elephants, Futteh Alli and Bundoola, as they are destined to reappear towards the end of this true history. Both animals are no doubt alive and well now, and their services are at the disposal of any sportsman who might like to give them another chance at tigers. But it was not during my next trip that I was to have the pleasure of testing Futteh Alli's pluck when confronted with a foe capable of retaliating his blows.

The chief native shikarries, Peyma and sons, being disengaged, I decided to once more visit the Neemuch country. The tigers, I knew, had been dreadfully reduced in numbers, but this objection applied to so many places, and at all events in these districts I should know the country and the people, which would give me a great advantage.

To Neemuch, therefore, I journeyed, and found everything much as I had left it two years before. The great Roghanath Guj was still the leading elephant of the place. He was, of course, to make one of the party, and I was to ride him. Then there was another tusk elephant, called Heera Guj, to carry the howdah for the two friends, Hilton and Purdey, who had kindly consented to go with me. A small female elephant, called Jobun Burree, who would only be expected to help in the beat, completed our number. I was naturally very glad to see my old friend Roghanath Guj again, and as soon as we had got clear of cantonments, and made our first halt in the jungle, I went up to him at his picket, and presented him with a large lump of his favourite goor. I was at once struck with the indifference with which he accepted this trifling mark of my esteem, for, during the preceding trip of two years ago, he had invariably devoured with avidity as much of this sweet stuff as he could get. The next day, his repugnance being still more marked, I spoke to the mahout Ghassee Ram about it, who said, 'It is because the weather is so hot that he has no taste for plain sugar, he wishes it to be mixed with ghee (grease made from butter).'

I accepted the hint, and next day I visited him with half a dozen balls made up according to the new recipe. But it was with difficulty that I could make him swallow one or two; he seemed to take them entirely to oblige me. I was sure there must be something wrong with the poor beast, but Ghassee Ram, who was his responsible keeper, was positive that all was right. I suggested toothache, but he declared that never had an elephant sounder teeth. I then asked if it might not be one of his periodical attacks of delirious fever coming on. 'That,' he said, 'I will answer for it, is quite impossible. For eighteen years I have lived with this elephant as his keeper, and he has never had an illness of that sort till the rains have well set in. No, no, sahib, you may believe me, there is nothing the matter with him. The heat of the weather makes him irritable, that is all.'

With such answers I was obliged to be satisfied, though I could not but remember that during our former trip the weather had been decidedly hotter, and that the elephant had always been quite lively and good-tempered. I could only suppose, then, that two years had gradually brought some slight changes even to so huge and solid a creature as Roghanath Guj. I consequently continued to treat him with confidence, and used daily to mount by his tusks to my accustomed seat behind his ears. I now began to notice that the mahout always kept him well apart from the other elephants, and that he was also secured for the night at some thirty yards away from them. Things went on in this way for some time, during which, in the absence unfortunately of any tigers, this elephant and his keeper were my chief objects of interest,—the one on account of his strange and sombre manner, the other by reason of his confident, yet to my mind utterly unsatisfactory, method of explaining the apparently critical state of his formidable charge.

One morning, after an unsuccessful beat, we had all assembled previous to shifting our ground. The elephants and beaters were to go in one direction, whilst we were to make a considerable detour in another. I mounted my pony and rode off, but was shortly rejoined by Hilton, who had witnessed the following scene. The elephant-keepers, with the exception of Ghassee Ram, had dismounted, and the animals, keepers, beaters, etc., were all standing about in a loose group, previous to proceeding to the new cover, when suddenly Roghanath Guj made a rush at mahout Himmat Khan, and pursued him, in spite of the efforts of Ghassee Ram to restrain him, till the former, in a moment of happy inspiration, flung his long-flowing turban on a bush which grew on the bank of a ravine, and himself slipped through the thorns and foliage into the watercourse below, where he lay *perdu*. The stratagem was successful. The elephant at once knelt on the bedecked bush, and having vented his rage harmlessly on the same, he behaved more placidly for the rest of the day.

I now thought seriously of sending the beast back to Neemuch, but did not see very well how to manage it, as it would entail a solitary march of about three days for the keeper, during which it was impossible to forecast what might happen. Should he break loose, it might be months before he could be either killed or recaptured. So, as Ghassee Ram still asserted positively that the elephant was only a little cross, and that he could by extra care guarantee that there would be no serious accident, I resolved that he should still continue with the party. After all it appeared quite as dangerous to send him away as to keep him, for there was no elephant like him for exploring perilous nooks and corners, or for settling a dangerous tiger.

The day after this questionable conduct on the part of

Roghanath Guj we found ourselves beating the very same ravine, called Ghātie, in which two years before I shot the second tigress from the head of the elephant. There was no doubt another tigress in this nullah, but she did not seem inclined to yield to the beat. I was just thinking of descending from my post, when she appeared before me roaring and bounding at a tremendous pace from rock to rock, as she fled wildly down the valley. I raised my smooth-bore gun and fired. The tigress uttered a sort of choking cough, and waved her right arm high in the air. But her speed, instead of being slackened, was greater than ever as she vanished down the steep and craggy descent. The elephants were now summoned in haste, my two friends were soon in the howdah, and I advanced to the head of the gloomy-looking Roghanath. I noticed then that his skin, especially about the face, appeared dry, pale, and withered; also, that Ghassee Ram could not conceal his anxiety as I placed my hands at the roots of his tusks, preparatory to mounting. The elephant, too, seemed reluctant to stoop for me, and the mahout begged me to ascend nimbly, and not to kick the animal's forehead with my boots, as that might irritate him. I ascended, however, in safety to my favourite eminence, on which I was no sooner seated than the elephant attempted the life of his under-keeper, whose name I have forgotten. The man escaped by springing on to a rock, and Roghanath Guj, obedient to my guiding touch, at once commenced the difficult descent, down which the tigress had just flown with the ease and almost the speed of a great bird.

Being unencumbered by a howdah, I got down into the comparatively smooth valley a little before the other elephant

Heera Guj, and soon came upon the bright body of the tigress lying at full length on a clear piece of ground. She was quite dead, the bullet having passed close to her heart as it traversed her body, and then struck the rocks beyond with a sound that had caused me to fear at the time that I must have missed. From her appearance as she lay before me, I suspected that she had cubs, so I caused a careful search to be made in all the likely places. This resulted in the discovery of the three beautiful little male cubs which have already been fully described on a former page, so I need only here add that on arriving at our tents a good milch-goat was procured as a foster-mother for the little orphans. She proved a very good nurse, and was inclined to like the little creatures, only they were so greedy, and used to scratch her so at feeding-time that their paws had to be held till they had taken enough.

Two days after securing these interesting pets we arrived at a small village which I am never likely to forget. It was called Mehra.

There was a great deal of very strong and wild jungle in the neighbourhood, and a freshly-killed pony testified to the presence of a tiger.

Close to the village were some enormous banyan trees, under which the elephants were secured. Opposite to them, on the other side of a small clearing, stood our little camp. Here, after a long and unsuccessful day's beating for the wary tiger, we had enjoyed our late dinner, and had just sought our couches, clad for the night in our light sleeping suits, when a sudden burst of affrighted cries broke upon our ears. The tumult proceeded from the direction of the great tree where Roghanath Guj stood in solitude.

We instantly rushed for our guns, and I seized a hurricane lamp. We made all haste in our slippered feet to the scene of action. As we got to within twenty yards of the elephant, Ghassee Ram called out to us to halt. The elephant, he said, was obeying him, and that if nothing further incensed him he would be able to lace up his hind legs with a rope, when he would be incapable of further mischief. So we stood where we were and waited in great anxiety, whilst we could hear the mahout uttering the word 'Sōm-sōm,' which is the order for the elephant to keep his hind quarters towards any one who may be washing or otherwise attending to him. The night was dark as pitch; nothing could be seen. According to the different cries, however, of the excited people, it was clear something had happened to the under-keeper of Roghanath Guj. Some said he was dead, others that he had escaped from his fearful assailant. I called to the other elephant-keepers, but they had all gone with their elephants, I knew not whither, at the first alarm. Perhaps the under-keeper was with them. Meanwhile Ghassee Ram was left quite alone to deal with the enraged beast. Of course, we talked to him all the time, and were prepared to rush in and fire as well as we could should he call to us to do so. Every chance, however, would have been against our disabling the elephant, who, maddened by such wounds as he might receive, would have worked untold destruction during the long dark hours of a moonless night. To the pluck of Ghassee Ram must be ascribed the avoidance of such a calamity. In a few minutes, which seemed an age, the mahout called out that we might advance. We did so, and never shall I forget the weirdness of the scene as it was lighted up by the bright rays of the lamp I carried. Under the tree, with his back to its stem, towered the dark form of the elephant, whilst the mahout, a mere speck, stood a little to the elephant's right. No other living thing was visible, but close to the elephant, on the opposite side to Ghassee Ram, lay a small and shapeless object, which a second glance showed to be the body of the missing man. The elephant, with his ears raised, seemed to be keeping guard over his fallen victim, and would perhaps kill any one who might attempt to remove the body, which was within reach of his trunk. Still, this must be done, and at once, for life might still be lingering in the shattered frame. I therefore gave the hurricane lamp to the mahout, and ordered him to swing it up into the elephant's face, and to call out his name at the same time. Ghassee Ram, from the long habit of commanding this huge animal, had acquired some powerful tones. As he swung the lamp which hung from a long ring in the elephant's face, and called out 'Roghanath Guj, Roghanath Guj,' the animal seemed deeply impressed. As the lamp ascended for the third time into his dazzled eyes, I darted from between my two friends, who stood covering the elephant with their guns, and drew forth the unfortunate keeper. He was terribly mangled, and quite dead. The elephant had put his foot on his head, so that his features were unrecognizable. All that remained now was to see to the safety of the elephant. The rope with which his hind legs were laced was very insecure, I thought, so I had fires lighted all round him, and plenty of watchers put on to call us at once if he showed signs of trying to break loose, in which case I should, of course, have felt bound to shoot him at once. Nothing, however, occurred during the night, but at the dawn of day I proceeded again to the fatal tree. There lay the chain that should have been round the elephant's front feet, but which the careless keepers, notwithstanding the uncertain state of the elephant, had thought it too much trouble to affix. The elephant was still looking much excited, and the two strange pores, one over each temple, which are invisible when the animal is in health, were now pouring forth a stream of some kind of liquid that ran, ever broadening, down the creature's face. This was a sure sign that the elephant was in prematurely for his annual fever, and would be unsafe to approach for two or three months to come. He still, however, seemed to recognize Ghassee Ram and myself, so together we induced him to lie down, and allow us to put on his handcuffs. This accomplished, I felt more comfortable, and now demanded an account of the circumstances attending this sad tragedy.

'Well, sahib,' said Ghassee Ram, 'the elephant was standing as I thought all right when the under-keeper passed by him to go and fetch some more fodder. Just as he was crossing, the elephant grasped him in his trunk, and dashed him to the earth. The man called out to me "Foujdar! Foujdar!" (*i.e.* keeper, keeper). I at once jumped up, and called out in a loud voice, "Roghanath Guj, what is this that you have done?" On my saying this, the elephant stood quite still for a few seconds, but the man was too much injured to make his escape, and the elephant then finished him.'

This was a very sad episode in a shikar trip, but it would

have been much worse if any one other than one of the animal's own keepers had been killed. They had persisted most obstinately that the beast was all right, so that the same catastrophe would certainly have occurred wherever the elephant might have been kept. Fortunately Ghassee Ram was a man of resources, and had procured a long stout rope, used to raise water from a neighbouring well. With this the elephant's hind legs were properly laced up, and he was really deprived of all power to do any further mischief. Still, I was determined to give up all idea of shooting, and to await the arrival of the elephant Mānut Dār, in quest of whom I had sent in a horseman to Neemuch. This elephant had at all times great influence over Roghanath Guj, and would be of great use in keeping him quiet till the worst was over, and after that in getting him to return quietly through the country on his way back to the cantonments. Whilst thus kept waiting, I could not but be touched by the affection this huge creature displayed, even in his madness, towards the only two people that he loved—Ghassee Ram and myself. Every day I fed him from my hand, and he never failed to clank his heavy chains, and turn round to watch me till I disappeared into my tent on leaving him. Poor Roghanath! I felt for him, notwithstanding his crimes, all of which he had committed while under the delirium of fever. At other times he was as gentle as a lamb and brave as a lion. As soon as Mānut Dār had arrived, who besides her own powers of soothing had brought fresh chains of great weight and strength, there was no reason for any longer delaying our shooting operations, so the next day we left Mehra, and bid adieu for ever to poor Roghanath Guj.

Could I but have foreseen the dreadfully cruel death that he was destined to suffer, I would certainly have shot him, and run the risk of having to pay the hundred pounds which was duly registered as his cost price. But we are not prophetic, so the doomed elephant had to die under circumstances much too painful to be recorded in these pages.

In judging of elephants and their characteristics, it should be borne in mind that ever since prehistoric times down to the present day, they have only existed as wild beasts in vast forests. Nowhere are they bred in captivity.

Roghanath Guj himself passed his early life amid regions surpassing in rugged wildness anything that I could describe, as all his ancestors had done before him for countless generations. How being caught, often at a mature age, and driven into captivity, they can in the course of a few months be transformed into such intelligent, docile, and affectionate servants, must strike any one with astonishment. Of course, it occasionally happens that one of the lady captives proves to be in an interesting condition at the time she is taken, and then a baby elephant makes its appearance in the heart of civilization. A very intelligent mahout once told me that these camp-bred animals are objected to by the fraternity of keepers, because they grow up as great pets, and never acquire that respect for man which is inculcated by the terrific experiences they go through at the time of being made prisoners. I have, I am sorry to say, never had an opportunity of assisting at the capture of any elephants, but most of us have read interesting accounts of such operations, and we can well imagine the stupefaction with which they must be filled on finding themselves firmly bound and secured chiefly by the efforts of their own kind. On the score, then, of their being possessed of absolutely no hereditary advantages, as regards their intercourse with man, I would claim the generous indulgence of my readers for such faults as I must confess they from time to time commit.

CHAPTER XIV.

ON leaving Mehra, our little party was reduced to two, as Purdey could not stay with us any longer. Hilton and I were therefore obliged to divide the ground as well as we could; but we often found ourselves much in want of a third gun. For some days we beat the jungle sedulously without seeing anything. Many reasons were given by our native shikarries to account for the scarcity of tigers; but the truth was, I suspect, that this country having once been full of these animals, had become so much frequented by shooting parties, that the big game had been almost exterminated. It was too late, however, to get to fresh jungles this year, so we tried to make up by hard work for all deficiencies.

One day, when we had almost exhausted our beaters, we decided upon making a final effort, by driving a large tract of scrub jungle. There were no trees or rocks to get upon, so we each lay down on the ground at a distance of about three hundred yards apart. We were soon left in complete solitude, as our guides left us, and went by a detour to join the beaters. Ere long the inspiriting sound of rough music was heard in the distance. The striking up of the band never fails to rouse the sportsman's interest and energies; no matter how many beats may have proved blank, there is the same chance as ever that the present one may turn out successful. In the present instance it was not long before I heard the crack of my friend's rifle, which was shortly followed by the appearance of a very large bear, shuffling along about thirty yards in front of me. He had a fine long black coat of his own, and, as it stood all on end with wrath, he seemed to tower above the bushes through which he was retreating. I aimed behind his shoulder, and sent a twelve-bore bullet right through his body. He fell in a heap, almost without a groan; but as he was waving his limbs about, I continued to cover him in case he should show signs of rallying. Before there was time for this point to be decided, I perceived Hilton running somewhat imprudently up to the fallen animal. Of course I hastened to support him in case of accidents. There was no need, however, of any further firing; a single bullet had proved sufficient to settle this powerful and healthy animal, although its heart had not been touched. We measured him as he lay on the ground, and found his length to be six feet one inch. As a bear has no tail worth mentioning, this length represents an animal of considerable size.

This beast was a very fine specimen of the sloth bear, which is, I think, the only variety of the ursine tribe that inhabits the plains of India proper. Though far inferior to the famous grizzly in height and weight, it is nevertheless a most formidable animal. It is of very massive structure, extremely muscular, and furnished with claws of immense length, which, if blunt, are quite sharp enough to bury themselves in the flesh of any antagonist that they may be able to close with. These bears are said by many to be strict vegetarians, and perhaps where they have a plentiful supply of whatever food they like best, they may be so; but it has always seemed to me as if the long canine fangs with which they are furnished must be intended to fit them for at least the occasional slaughter of other beasts. My opinion on this head was strengthened when, on once visiting a celebrated menagerie at feeding-time, I saw these animals served with a meal of raw meat, and nothing else, just the same as the rest of the carnivora, and they devoured with greedy relish what was given to them. Their appearance, however, was such as to warrant a suspicion that they were not properly managed, as they were not more than half the size of their wild relations, and were besides almost destitute of hair; in short, they were pitiable objects.

The day after shooting the large bear as above described, we tried another branch of the same jungle, in hopes of meeting with more of the family. We had not sat long in the trees during the first beat when I heard my friend fire, which was followed by a terrific and prolonged roaring. Thinking something might have happened to Hilton, I scrambled to the ground, and ran up to his position. I found him gone, but, directed by the row, I soon came up with him. A wounded bear was in front of us, but it soon ceased its cries, and though we tracked it by the blood for a mile and a half at least, we were unable to come up with it and its two companions. It seems that three bears had come down the nullah, but had made such good use of the rocks and bushes that Hilton, though a very good shot, had never been able to get a really good view of any of them.

At first we had great hopes of coming up with the wounded beast, but our head shikarrie, Rama, said, 'We shall never overtake them; for when a bear makes such a prodigious noise as this one did, it is a sure sign that it is only slightly hurt and greatly enraged.' And Rama proved to be right; for though we tracked them to where they had crossed an open space of some miles, we never saw them again.

Our next interview with bears was more fortunate. Hilton had been told off to sit on a narrow ledge of black rock, with a nice jungle spread out before him. As he sat with his feet dangling unsuspiciously over a narrow crevice, the rock underneath him suddenly began to vibrate with much scuffling and growling. He had just time to whip up his feet when a bear of unusually large size contrived to bolt from underneath them, and out of the very crack which at first sight seemed too small to admit of the passage of so large a body. My friend despatched him with one shot, and was much pleased with his capture, as the beast was in remarkably fine coat, and measured six feet three inches.

Tigers, as I have said before, proved scarce during this expedition, so that it was more than usually mortifying to see and not kill one. During one beat that we had about this time I saw a tiger making off from behind where we were posted, as we had not been placed far enough back. I might have taken a long shot with my Express rifle had I not seen Rama slip immediately from his tree, and vanish among the bushes. Of course I thought he was going to signal to stop the beat, and then make arrangements for heading the tiger by making a long detour. In this belief I sat, with constantly diminishing patience, expecting sudden silence to ensue; but instead of this the line advanced, with everything going on at concert pitch, till it arrived at my very feet.

Every one having arrived except Rama, I inquired where he was, and found he was pursuing the tiger by himself, with nothing but a long stick in his hand. However he was perfectly safe, for with such a noise behind him the tiger was not likely to stop till he had reached some other lair, perhaps ten miles off. It was strange that an experienced head shikarrie should have acted in such a foolish manner; but even weasels, I suppose, are sometimes caught napping.

On another occasion, I and Hilton had been placed in trees rather near together, with a narrow stream of water running between us. We had agreed that he should take the first shot on whose side of the stream the tiger should make his appearance. Thus we sat in our earth-coloured clothes, moving nothing but our eyes. Mine shortly encountered those of a large tiger glaring at me from the midst of a thick bush. Nothing could be seen except its great round face, with the yellow eyes intently fixed upon me. I stirred not a muscle; if I raised the gun, the beast would probably vanish on the instant. Besides, it was not on my side of the stream, so that I was bound in every way to keep quite still, in hopes that it might advance in the desired direction. My policy was to a certain extent successful, for in a few moments it burst from its cover, and rushed with lightning speed towards me. I just waited to hear Hilton take the first shot, and then fired myself at the animal's retreating form as it vanished into a swamp abounding with pools and bushes. A well-marked trail of blood showed that the tiger was hit, and it seemed likely he would make a stand in such a nice cool retreat. My friend therefore took his place in the howdah, and in the absence of Roghanath Guj I got on the neck of the poor little female elephant, Jobun Burree. We were soon half-swimming, half-wading through all kinds of cover in this picturesque glen. Jobun Burree was quite unfit for the work; and had the tiger sprung at her when wallowing in a deep and slushy pond, it would not have surprised me had she actually died of fright. Entire ignorance of danger, however, kept her quite happy, and she plunged with great enjoyment into all the most dangerous places, in the somewhat mistaken belief that she was taken there to bathe. The tiger, however, crept away unperceived, and was seen in the distance crossing a stony hill. We at once dismounted from the elephants, and made every effort to intercept him before he could get to the main river, for which we now knew he was making. As he was lame, and dragging a hind leg after him, we seemed to have a good chance of this. I shall never forget the climb I had on this occasion. The mountains were lofty, and as nearly as possible perpendicular. But that was not all; bamboo trees contrived to grow upon them, and their fallen leaves rendered the surface as slippery as ice. Yet here I was invited by my native friends to run very fast. To do them justice, they seemed quite equal to this feat themselves. But I could only gasp, and vainly wish that it had fallen to Hilton's lot to travel by this route instead of me. His path, envy whispered to me, was probably ever so much better. However, I got to the top at last, and before me lay the track by which it was supposed the tiger was retreating. Whether I had got there too late, or whether the cunning brute had chosen another line, continues to this day a matter of speculation. Certain it is, that none of us ever saw him again.

Had we been content to shoot bears, we could no doubt have made a good bag, but we doubted the wisdom even of firing at them when we happened to meet with them; for being so much easier to find than tigers, the shikarries would have been only too glad to take us after them instead of pursuing the nobler animal. Bears are more independent of water than tigers, and for other reasons do not make the same districts their headquarters; so that to go after the one beast is to partially abandon the other. We therefore impressed upon Rama that we would rather shoot one tiger than all the bears in India. This being distinctly understood, we had no objection to dispose of such bears as might be found in, or on our way to, tiger jungles.

Accordingly, when Rama informed us that by going only two or three miles out of our way, he could show us a cave that was inhabited by bears, we were very glad to visit the spot. A beat was not in this case considered desirable, as these bears used to lie among the loose rocks all day in front of their subterranean home. We were therefore to try and creep up upon them so quietly as to be on them before they had time to dash into their holes. All this being settled, we started for the scene of action. After threading our way over some very rough hills and valleys, a steep and craggy range appeared suddenly in front of us. Rama now came to a halt, and said, 'The cave is among the rocks that form the abrupt ridge all along the top of yonder mountains. We must leave the elephants and beaters here, as even the most remote sound is sufficient to drive these creatures into their deep and extensive caves for the rest of the day; and then we may say good-bye to them. All the wood in the forest would not suffice to smoke them out. Their galleries are most extensive, and some of the outlets may be as much as a quarter of a mile distant; I will therefore go with you, and Goolba shall accompany Hilton, sahib; every one else must stay here. And as we four get nearer and nearer, we shall have to take more and more care not to make the slightest sound, else we shall have all our trouble for nothing.'

Now these injunctions may sound as simple and easy as others that I had received,—such as to climb, with my gun hanging round my neck, to the height of sixty feet up a forest tree, or to run very fast up the almost perpendicular side of a mountain; but when it comes to practice, these things have a nasty way of turning into impossibilities. In the present instance I knew that as soon as we got to really close quarters, Rama and Goolba would slip off their shoes, and really be able to advance with the stealthiness of cats. But we could not do this, as at the very first step our flesh would have stuck to the burning rocks. Even had we come provided with several pairs of thick stockings, there would still have been the thorns to contend with, and which would be comparatively powerless against the hardened soles of our dusky allies. With such somewhat discouraging forebodings, we started on our difficult enterprise. Whilst we were yet distant, everything was very enjoyable. We could walk at our usual pace in Indian file, and even converse in an ordinary tone of voice, till we came to the foot of the final declivity, at the top of which, immediately under some frowning rocks, the caves were situated. Here we began to go very slowly, looking to each step so as to avoid such things as loose stones or dried leaves and twigs. This naturally became more and more difficult to manage as we got deeper and deeper into the thick woods with which this rough mountain-side was covered. How I envied the snake-like movements of Rama and Goolba, who, with their sandals in their hands, glided beside us like those good children who are only seen, not heard!

For a long time things really had gone on better than I had expected, as far as I and Hilton were concerned. We had managed to make little or no noise with our booted feet. Still, our patience was severely tried, and mine almost broke down when our guides, on rounding some bushes, stood stock-still, with their fingers on their lips, and pointed upwards over a fearful heap of stones and boulders of rock which some convulsion of nature had hurled from their original resting-place above, and which now lay piled in front of us like a vast, loose avalanche of heterogeneous composition.

'The bears,' whispered Rama below his breath, 'are sleeping amongst this.'

For a moment despair seized me, and I stood rooted to the spot. Above could be dimly made out the arched entrance to the caves, into which these creatures would certainly rush at the first sound of alarm. How, then, were we to get over all this debris without at once rousing them from their siesta? As there were no certain means of accomplishing this feat, there was nothing for it but to gather our breath and our resolution, and commence the experiment. By observing every possible precaution, we got about three parts of the journey over without betraying ourselves. At this point, however, a treacherous stone gave way under somebody's feet. This was instantly followed by a sound of scuffling and tumbling just on the other side of a large stone, about five feet high, on my left. I scrambled on to the top of it as fast as I could, and could just distinguish a mass of black hair showing glimpses of itself as it passed rapidly through openings amongst the boulders, on its way to the comparatively open ground below.

By the time we had alarmed the bear we were slightly above him, so he probably thought he would be safer in flying into the forest than in endeavouring to take shelter in the cave. Besides, he could not have known exactly who were his enemies. The falling of the loose stone might portend the attack of a rival of his own species. In such a case to run to earth would prove a fatal mistake. At any rate, whatever motives may have actuated him, he made at his best pace down the mountain-side, and when at a distance of about thirty yards, he pulled up behind a thick bush, as though trying to make out who or what might be these intruders on his peace.

I fired at his indistinct form, and before I could see through the smoke to pull the second trigger, he was gone at a great pace, the bystanders said. We all ran after him as hard as we could, but with little hopes of overtaking him.

We stopped for a moment to look for signs of blood, but none were visible. It was just decided that I must have missed this haystack, when a poor, melancholy little squeak struck upon our ears. 'That,' exclaimed Goolba, 'is the well-known bear's death-cry; we shall soon come upon his dead body.' And, sure enough, before we had gone another twenty yards, we saw him lying quite still on the ground. Life was extinct when we got up to him, and we were glad to find that he was a fine specimen, with rich, long black fur, and measuring the same as the former one that fell to my gun, namely six feet one inch.

Whilst we were still in this neighbourhood, our shikarries informed us that there was a panther inhabiting some steep rocks and bushes at the back of a village called Palkas, to which place we consequently repaired.

When we saw the locality, we could not believe any wild beast could inhabit it, as the cover it was said to live in was close to the village, and the country all round was very open. However, we took up the posts assigned for us, each on a tree about a hundred and fifty yards apart, and the whole country around as open as a race-course. All the beaters and villagers now went to the top of the rocks where dwelt the panther, and simultaneously launched a shower of stones down the steep slope. This volley was accompanied by every noise that previous thought and ingenuity could devise. The effect was certainly splendid of its kind, and resulted in a very fine panther quitting this stronghold, tearing at a racing pace across the plain, and passing exactly midway between our two trees.

We fired I am afraid to say how many shots, but we had evidently miscalculated the effect of his great speed, for all of them missed. On getting down and examining the ground, one bullet mark at all events was found in the centre of one of his footprints. Probably we had never aimed sufficiently in front of him, and so lost our prize.

We were now in a more open country, approaching, in fact,

the borders of the jungle, and consequently also the end of our trip. Still, there were some good places to be visited, and the beats were more interesting in one respect than in the thicker covers, as one could see the animals on the move long before they got up to the posts. They would vanish, and then reappear somewhat nearer. Or perhaps they would try to head in some other direction, when a well-placed scout would earn a blessing by uttering a terrific yell from an elevated rock or tree, and the victim would resume his former course.

One day I was sitting in a solitary tree that commanded an extensive view of the vast cup-shaped valley below, when I saw a bear nearly a mile off, working his way in front of the beaters. Sometimes he would stop, and listen attentively to the beat coming on in a long line behind him. Then again he would trot on a bit, or he would disappear in some deep ravine that intersected the valley; and just as I was speculating on whether he had decided to rush frantically along the bottom of this watercourse, and thus turn the line of beaters, he would reappear with a great bounce, the result of his charging up the steep bank of the nullah. Once he made a great effort to turn to his left, and get out of the valley on a line that would have ensured his escape, but there was fortunately a party at this point to turn him. So on he came nearer and nearer, till I could watch every step he made. At last, when at about fifty yards from me, he turned a little to get round a bush, thus giving me a good view of his right shoulder. I did not think it prudent to refuse this chance, as he might see me now at any moment, when he would, of course, break back as hard as he could go.

Now few people can be relied upon to hit with the rifle an animal flying at great speed amongst bushes, long grass, and other cover, so I took the opportunity now presented, and planted a bullet from my smooth-bore gun within an inch or so of the spot I had aimed at, behind the right shoulder. Instead, however, of falling dead on the spot, the brute charged with unusual speed to the foot of the small leafless tree in which I was sitting. I thought he meant to climb up to me, in which case I could best have despatched him by putting a bullet through his head at close quarters, to which end I reserved my second shot. He was not, however, up to this effort, so he merely ran on another twenty yards or so, and then dropped down dead.

He turned out to be a large male animal, more than six feet in length, but with the exception of his head and shoulders, which were well coated, the rest of his fur was not good.

After this we came to our last halting-ground, where our pleasant trip was to come to an end. Notwithstanding the dearth of tigers, we had enjoyed our outing thoroughly. After all, we had bagged one tigress, three cubs, and four large bears, which we considered quite worth coming into the jungle for.

Peepun was the name of the village where we drove the jungle for the last time, and although we did not succeed in adding to our little bag, we witnessed one of those curious instances of exceptional conduct, on the part of wild animals, which are so instructive to those who, from motives of sport or science, are interested in studying their habits.

The jungle here was widespread, and ran irregularly up innumerable watercourses and ravines, between which lay open or even bald tracts of considerable extent. As I sat attentively watching the surrounding country, I saw at a considerable distance from me a large sambur deer emerge from a deep thicket, and cross a perfectly open space. Almost touching her heels, followed a very much lower animal, which for some time I hardly looked at, believing it to be her fawn. They had taken the alarm in good time, and were wending their way at a foot's pace along a narrow jungle track. When one stopped, the other did the same. What, then, was my surprise when a sudden movement of the hinder animal showed me that it was a panther. Whether these two animals had formed a permanent friendship, or whether the suspicion of danger had united them for the time only, I could not say. Certain it is that they walked off calmly together, and disappeared into the next nullah.

This instance of strange companionship was not only seen by a large number of the scouts and beaters, but also by Hilton, who was so much nearer to them than myself that he had some thoughts of taking a long shot at the panther. But, of course, as they were quietly retreating into another ravine full of dense cover, it was much better to let them settle into that, and make preparations for another drive. This we did, but though we worked hard for this our last day, we neyer saw either of the animals again.

Nightfall saw us once again in Neemuch, where we speedily dismissed Rama, Goolba, and the rest of the shikarries engaged for the trip.

It is almost impossible to make sure of choosing well the country you will shoot over during the ensuing season. A tract that is well known as holding many tigers may prove to be shot out, or another party may get the start of you. If, on the other hand, you decide upon striking out a new line for yourself, there can be no means of forecasting the results. The native shikarries of any particular jungle cannot be expected to sacrifice their own interests by telling you they have nothing to show you, and that you had better, therefore, go elsewhere. Owing to these and other such-like considerations, the lover of big-game shooting suffers much from doubt and anxiety before committing himself to the start.

Once under way, nothing remains but to make the best of everything. One's idea of what *is* the best may vary considerably, according to individual notions. For instance, when it was seen that tigers were so scarce, and so difficult to get a sight of, Rama suggested that we should make bears and sambur stags our chief objects. He said he could take us to plenty of jungles where both these animals were very numerous, and I have no doubt, had we acceded to this proposition, we should have got at least a dozen good specimens of each. But we had gone out to shoot tigers, and no smaller game would satisfy us.

CHAPTER XV.

BUT although our arrival at Neemuch marked the end of the great effort at tiger-shooting for that year, still, owing to the proximity of suitable jungle, and the apparent holding off of the monsoon, there was still a possibility of making a fresh start on ten days' leave, if I could get it. I therefore retained everything that was required to enable me to be off at a moment's notice, such as camels to carry the kit, and hired ponies for the use of my servants. I never make my domestics walk on the march, as after a long tramp they cannot be fit to discharge their duties on arrival at the new camp. Besides, on an expedition of pleasure, all should, if possible, enjoy themselves.

I did not think much of the elephant, Heera Guj, who had hitherto borne the howdah, and Roghanath was still suffering the pangs of delirium in all its force. So I procured another heavy tusker, called Ashmut Guj, who at any rate looked a match for any tiger, for my own riding, and designed Heera for any one who might go with me and like to use the howdah.

I got the desired leave, and set off at once, by myself, for a place called Gungarar, about forty miles from Neemuch, and on the high road to Nusseerabad. Every one said there were tigers in this jungle, which had been undisturbed for a long time. The native shikarries avoided this neighbourhood as much as possible, as there was hardly a tree in the entire district, nor yet a rock up which a tiger could not spring with ease. No doubt this rendered the sport dangerous both to the sportsman and the beaters, and under ordinary circumstances I would have chosen a less perilous country. But the time was short, so it must be Gungarar or nowhere. Owing to there being a good road to the place, I got out in one night to it, and found a very nice little travellers' bungalow to live in on the very borders of the jungle. There was an extremely civil man in charge, called Roopa, of whom more anon.

This being quite out of the territorial limits of the worthy family of Rama, I was without any shikarrie; so, agreeably to recommendations I had received, I sent to the adjacent village for a man called Hurrichund, who, it was said, would organize a beat, and without whom I might not count on the beaters turning out, as they were difficult to get here. Hurrichund promptly obeyed my summons. He was a tall, thin man with rather bandy legs, light grey, almost blue eyes, and, as I saw afterwards on a striking occasion, a tonsured skull garnished only with a surrounding fringe of long tawny hair. He had once been a Government elephant-keeper, but on seeing an elephant, I think it was Roghanath Guj, trample some one to death, he had retired from that business, 'and,' added Roopa with some contempt, 'he has not recovered his nerve to this day!' However, I had to make the best of Hurrichund, and everything was arranged to have a beat the next day at eleven o'clock.

Punctually as the hour came, we all started for the

favourite locality of a tiger that was well known to be never very far off, and who had even been seen at night-time to enter the enclosure of the travellers' bungalow where I was now living. Hurrichund advised me to visit some of the thickest patches of corinda bush on the elephant to start with, as the beaters would not enter them. This I proceeded to do on the neck of Heera Guj. There appeared to be nothing in the immediate vicinity, so I pulled up, and began to consider what should be done next, when suddenly the tiger charged from behind at the elephant, who was so terrified that he fled at once at a gallop, a pace which elephants are not supposed to be capable of, and perhaps it may require a tiger at their heels to enable them to do it, as this one certainly did. The tiger, having put us to flight, disappeared, and could not be seen again, so another expedition was planned for the next day. Meanwhile, a shooting acquaintance of mine arrived at the bungalow, and volunteered to accompany me.

Having arrived at the ground, I at once dismounted from the elephant, and went, guided by two natives who each *said* he had shot many tigers, to a high spot near the top of a hill, where the scrub bush had almost ceased to grow. I lay down, with my two natives behind me, on a perfectly smooth and open piece of ground, across which it was supposed the tiger might be driven. Below me, at a distance of three hundred yards, I could see my friend Grove standing in the howdah borne by Ashmut Guj; and he, notwithstanding the distance, could see plainly our little party. My post commanded a good view, not only to the front, but also across a gorge to my left, the slope of which on my side was much too steep for me to see down it, and the lower part of it was densely covered with bushes.

Soon after the commencement of the beat, I had the pleasure of seeing the tiger coming slowly towards me on the opposite slope of the gorge to my left. I had no intention of firing at him till he had crossed over and got close up to me, as he was quite a hundred and fifty yards from me. Unfortunately my friend's views of the shikar were not quite the same as my own, for although he was at a still greater distance, he fired at the animal, and missed, for I distinctly heard the bullet strike the hard and rocky ground considerably short of the tiger, who turned quite round, and was preparing to break back among the beaters. There was nothing for it, then, but for me to fire, which I did with my Express rifle just as he was passing a solid wall of rock. My bullet passed close over his head, and struck the hard stone just in front of his face. Fragments of lead and flint must have been splashed into his very eyes. He turned in fury, and saw whence the attack was coming. Headlong he descended his slope, and began ascending mine at the same pace, uttering short sharp roars at each bound. To do myself justice, I must say I felt perfectly cool, and prepared to take aim calmly, no matter what his aspect might be on bounding into our little clearing. I merely flattened myself on the earth, which was the same colour as my clothes, and felt confident I should see the tiger before he saw me. Alas! I had forgotten the existence of the two natives.

At this critical moment, when the tiger was within thirty yards, and charging at his utmost speed right upon us, I heard a faint voice say, 'Khudawand (my lord), what are your orders?' I glanced backward. Heavens! what a sight greeted my unprepared eyes! My two aides-de-camp had positively *got up*, and were standing erect. Their faces were distorted, and they were executing a sort of subdued jumping. What, reader, I ask you, was I to do? Was it likely they would flatten themselves, and remain motionless? This was the line of conduct I had already ordered, and which they had abandoned. Not a stone, not a bush was near that could afford them an asylum, and if there had been they could not have moved a step to it without me. There was just one line leading over the round, smooth knoll on which we were, which I judged was sufficiently sloped to hide us if we ran as hard as we could instantaneously. There was not a second to reflect on whether I would sacrifice my dignity or the lives of those two natives. I chose the former course, and just as we disappeared at full speed, Grove saw the tiger land on the spot we had quitted. The slope of the ground being so very even, it was impossible to guess when we had retreated just far enough, so that when I turned and cautiously advanced my head over the rising ground, on the chance that the tiger might be trying to make out where we were, he was no longer visible, and had either gone onwards or descended again into the thick valley below. This, though annoying, was after all for the best, as I must confess that my nerves were no longer firm. It was the first time I had ever run away, and I had never thought about fright or whether it was contagious. I think, if I had ever had to run away again, my business-like feelings would have stood the test. As it was, they soon recovered sufficiently to have another beat; but the jungle was so spreading, that it was quite impossible to guess by which point of the compass the tiger might go, and we saw him break nearly a quarter of a mile off.

Of course this was a very black day in my annals, but the tiger would never leave this jungle, so the game was still alive, and I resolved that nothing short of the termination of my leave should separate us. On my way home I was very much amused at a conversation that I overheard amongst those who were following us. Said a voice in subdued accents, 'He will never shoot this tiger, never, for it is not a tiger but a faqueer (holy man) who has long ago quitted the human shape, and is doomed to accomplish the rest of his penance in the form of a wild beast. Till this is done, the higher powers will protect him. As a proof that what I say is true, the bangles which the saint wore on his arms are still around the tiger's wrists.'

At this an awed silence fell upon the audience, which was broken at last by one who still preserved some freedom of thought.

'Have you yourself ever seen these ornaments on this tiger?' said the doubter.

'Hundreds of times,' responded the voice. This closed the subject effectually, and the silence was not again broken.

On arriving at the bungalow, my friend was obliged to leave me, so I had now to continue my operations alone till the end of my leave. Knowing nothing whatever of the men under me, was of course a great drawback; it is so difficult to know what anybody will be like till he has had a trial. I had begun, however, to think a very great deal of Roopa, the care-taker of the bungalow, and we had many private talks together. He said, 'You see, Hurrichund is not up to the mark, but he has great influence in the village, and could easily persuade the beaters not to turn out. He will not give up, because he likes the money that is going about on these occasions, so it will not do to quarrel with him. To-morrow, however, I will go with you as your gun-bearer to one of the most favoured haunts of this tiger, and I think we shall be sure to see him, however badly the beat may be conducted.'

In pursuance of this plan, we proceeded next day to the other side of the shallow lake, which formed an important feature in this country, and arrived at some large black-looking stones close to its margin, and threaded in various directions by the beaten tracks of the tiger. Under the shelter of these stones we sat, and watched the surrounding bushes. Soon the sounds of the beat were heard, and shortly after Roopa and I simultaneously saw the tiger distinctly among the leafless bushes, at not more than thirty yards from us. It was motionless, and we also stirred not. I hardly liked to fire, for although the shrubs, being stripped of foliage, one could see plainly through them, yet there was many a thick stump between me and the tiger, any one of which might cause my bullet either to strike falsely or miss altogether. I should therefore much have preferred waiting for the animal to come on a little, but as he had seen us, and was staring hard at the tops of our heads, I could not expect that he would do this. I whispered my anxious doubts to Roopa, who said, 'Fire of course.' On this, as I was covering the beast, I pulled the trigger, which was followed by a frightful roar, and a plunging and tumbling among the bushes in front of us. We both rushed to the front, as we feared for the safety of the beaters. The tiger, however, had taken an upward course, and had left tracks of blood behind him, so I mounted the head of Ashmut Guj, and began ascending the slope in the direction he had taken, but could not find him.

There was a cave close by, and it was thought he might have retreated into it, so I got off the elephant, and having constructed a lay figure, by means of a large elephant cloth and some brushwood, I got to the top of the cave and dangled this object in front of its entrance. But nothing responded to these wiles, so, with a final jerk, I caused the scarecrow to fly violently upwards, and it fell with a flop just behind me. The elephants thought it was now all up with us, and that the tiger was upon me. In an instant they turned, and fled wildly up the steep ascent. In their panic they were ready to use their trunks, anything, in fact, to save their lives. They swiped frantically at everything that they thought they saw in their paths, which luckily consisted only of inanimate objects, as, for fear of the wounded tiger, we had sent every one away except the two mahouts, myself, and Roopa. Eventually a stiff line of rocks stopped the retreating giants, who, however, would recognize no one for the rest of the day except the mahouts and myself. On this occasion, at any rate, I was of real use in managing them. We now went down in front of the cave, and found that the blood spots had gone on beyond it, so we continued the search in other directions as long as daylight lasted; but though the wounded beast was probably close by, we could not fall in with him, so I had to return once more unsuccessful to the bungalow. Roopa, on whom I now thoroughly relied, as being both intelligent and fearless, even to a fault, now advised me to give this tiger a rest, and proceed next day to a village three miles distant, called Solinga Ka Keri, close to which were known to be a tiger, tigress, and cub. The former was said to be a very formidable beast, and had rendered the jungle impracticable for camels, many of whom he had killed, and, with the aid of his family, devoured.

On arriving the next day at this village, it turned out to consist only of two or three uninhabited and ruined huts. The place did very well, however, for the elephants and beaters to 'rendezvous' at whilst the chief shikarries were deciding on the plans for beating. The jungle maintained the same character as at Gungarar, namely undulating hills, which were only steep in a few places; no trees or rocks, nothing, in fact, but low bushes. These were plentiful, and in many places so dense that in spite of their leafless state at this time of the year, you could not see more than a foot or so into them. Solinga Ka Keri stood on a wide and comparatively open slope, which terminated in a plain of irregular shape, which, considering the nature of the country, might be called extensive. A narrow brook, the drain from the surrounding hills, flowed along the lowest level, and even at the driest time of the year, supplied ample drinking water for all the denizens of the forest. On the banks of this stream grew a babul thorn, and under the thorn lay the body of a dead cow, killed and partly consumed by the tigers during the past night. There could be little doubt, after this, that the animals were lying gorged close at hand.

'Come with me at once,' said Roopa; 'I will take you to the proper place to sit, whilst Hurrichund goes off with the beaters and elephants.' We started together, and arrived at a narrow gorge between two hills. This gorge was literally stuffed with underwood of all sorts, many kinds of which were in full leaf,—a safe and delicious retreat for tigers. A pathway so narrow that two could not walk abreast, led into this solitary glen, but Roopa led the way without being in the least impressed for about fifty yards. He then turned sharp to the left, and said, 'We must ascend the gorge on this side till we can see over the cover and on to the opposite slope.' This we did, and soon gained a spot whence we could get the desired view. 'There,' said Roopa, 'the tigers will come out just in front of us across that little opening. The cub will most likely come first, and the parents will follow. I will pull your sleeve when the great male appears, for we must get him first at any rate.' All this, of course, was quite right, and made me feel the only mistake about Roopa was that I had not met with him long ago. Soon the beat was heard advancing, loud, discordant, but inspiriting withal.

Every moment we expected to see the tigers. Perhaps they might be sleeping close to us, and suddenly spring almost upon us. It was on the cards, and, though neither showed it, our nerves must have been strung to a high pitch. What then was our disgust, after all this excitement, when the beaters appeared on the opposite side of the gorge without having driven to us a single animal of any kind. Then, indeed, Roopa lost his phlegm.

Oh,' he said, 'that Hurrichund, see what he has done!

instead of going on an elephant through the thick cover on the side of the hill, he has coasted round it, and allowed all the beaters to do the same. Of course the tigers have broken back; what else should they do? But I know they live here, and to-morrow I will lead the beat; you shall sit here by yourself, and I will stake my life I will drive them up to you, but it must be for to-morrow, they have most likely gone a long way off for the present.'

'That is all very well,' I said, 'but how am I to get through to-day without any more shikar?'

'Well,' said Roopa, 'there is a moon up to nine o'clock to-night, so if you like I will make a comfortable machān (ambush) for you in the fork of the thorn over the dead cow. If you get into it at about three in the afternoon, and we all clear out of the jungle, and everything is kept quiet from that hour, they will very likely return to the dead cow some time before the moon sets; and you will get a shot quite close, but you will have to sit alone, as the thorn will not hold two.'

I agreed to this, and really a very comfortable, roomy nest, about ten feet from the ground, was soon made for me.

At three o'clock I prepared to ascend to my station, when one of the leading natives endeavoured to dissuade me.

'Sahib,' he said, 'you will be killed if you do this, or at any rate frightened to death like my poor brother. He once got into a high tree with two friends for this very purpose, and sure enough at about midnight the tigers came. One of the party fired at them and missed, when the tigers, who are always bold at night, roared with fury, and both of them made desperate efforts to ascend the tree. They would not desist during the whole night, and only went away when it got light. My unfortunate brother,' added the narrator, 'has never recovered the shock of what he went through on that occasion.'

This was not exactly a cheerful story, but I did not believe these tigers would act as those did in the above story. Besides, if you are safe up a tree, it must be a very good thing if the tigers try to climb it, as in doing so they would be very easy to shoot. However, I mention the story to show that there are natives of India who can feel anxious as to the fate of a white man, even when he is a stranger.

I thanked the poor man kindly for his good intentions, and was soon left in complete solitude in the wilderness. I was not uncomfortable, as, in addition to a good seat, boughs had been arranged over my head to keep the sun off, and to enable me to move a little without being seen. Neither was I dull, for I should not have been surprised at any moment after the people had all gone if the tigers had come prowling towards the banquet which remained to be finished.

Nothing, however, came, nor did any living thing venture to show itself on this tiger-haunted plain during the whole afternoon. Night fell, but the stillness remained unbroken. No distant roaring, no near footfall greeted my listening ear. I waited till the setting of the moon, when, as it became pitch dark, it would have been no use trying to shoot, even if the tigers had come. So I clambered down from the tree, and soon met Roopa, who, on the moon setting, had started on an elephant to fetch me.

The next morning early we again visited the spot, and found every bit of the cow gone. At some period of the night the revellers had assembled, and had no doubt enjoyed their good cheer.

The time had now come to see what could be done by a change of management, and it was decided on the morning of our second arrival that Roopa should lead the beat, whilst a native woodman should guide me again to the spot in the gorge which I had previously occupied. There were so many ravines to be crossed before reaching it, that I might miss the way if I went by myself. Besides, I required some one to carry my spare gun and leather bag of drinking water, etc.

CHAPTER XVI.

ALL being ready, my guide stepped forward, and at once led the way. As I followed him I could not help being struck with his picturesque and characteristic appearance. He was a very fine young man, and carried himself remarkably well. His raiment was close-fitting and scanty, giving no hold to the thorns that overhung our narrow path. His swift, firm steps were quite noiseless, owing to his naked feet, as he flitted on in front of me. Over one shoulder he carried my gun, whilst on the other was slung my drinking water. In his right hand he grasped the never-failing companion of all these people, a tiny little axe, the wooden handle of which is strong, and the small head heavily weighted. They are so dexterous in the use of this little instrument, that they sometimes overrate their estimate of what they can do with it. I have no doubt my friend thought he might split a tiger's skull with it, but I should have been very sorry to see him put to the test.

Well, on we went; and as the jungle thickened, I must have presented an unfavourable contrast to my light-stepping guide. Never had I met with so many crooked varieties of thorns. Of course I wore my formidable solar hat on my head, the outside of which consisted of a thickly-wadded cover, which projected well down the back. From the way the bushes persecuted this seemingly inoffensive object, one would have thought they were endowed with life, intelligence, and an evil spirit. No matter how liberally I calculated the distance on going through gaps, some vicious twig, or a whole bunch of them, would descend like a whip on my crown, and bury their fangs in the soft wool, without whose protection I could not encounter the rays of the sun. These little difficulties, however, were nothing more than a salutary trial of temper, and perhaps even served a useful purpose in preventing the attention from any momentary wanderings.

We followed a different track to the one I had gone by the preceding day, so that I did not know exactly where I was till my guide stepped quickly to one side, and politely signed to me to go first up the densely-wooded pathway through the gorge which I have already described. We had not gone far when our muffled footsteps started a large animal close to us on our right. At the first crash, however, I knew it to be a sambur deer by the noise of its hoofs on the dry ground, so that I did not even bring my gun to my shoulder, but continued onwards to the point where we were to turn up the slope to the left. We had hardly done this, and gained about half the required elevation, when a heavy body rustled away out of a dense patch of broad green leaves close to us. I knew from the sound that it was at least one of the tigers, and that my chances of seeing them were therefore much diminished. I decided, however, to let the beat take its course; so my guide, by skilfully bending down the top of a green and leafy bush, made an excellent little covered seat for me to sit in, and raised about two feet from the ground, so that, should I not kill the tiger outright, he might still fail to see and kill me.

These little arrangements being completed, my friend took leave of me, and, choosing the most open ground he could find, made his way back to Roopa to let him know that I was fixed in my position, and that the beat could commence. I was in full view and good command of the open space the tigers were intended to cross; but as the distance was, as far as I could judge, a hundred yards, and no bushes intervened, I judged it best to use my Express rifle, and with this I sat waiting as the beat, ably conducted by Roopa, slowly approached me. How shall I describe my feelings when I suddenly saw a magnificently bearded and muscular tiger stalk slowly into the centre of the little clearance, as though in obedience to the expressed commands of the excellent Roopa! If, after so much waiting and so many disappointments, my hand had trembled at this supreme moment, perhaps I might have been excused; but as I aimed behind his shoulder, I felt sure of myself. I pulled the trigger, and with a movement swifter than the eye could follow, this kingly beast was lying on his back, with his head and feet contracted together in convulsive agony.

I had just time to think, 'Well, he is done for,' when, with an equally sudden motion, he was up again and behind some bushes. I gave him the contents of my second barrel at once; but though the bullet proved to have struck well forward, it seemed to have no effect upon him, as he kept on making short runs among the underwood. I now put down my rifle on to the ground, which I could reach, and took up my smooth-bore just as the beaters showed on the opposite brow of the overhanging gorge. The tiger, incredible as it may seem, endeavoured to charge them, and sent them all chattering back except one man, who found a thorn of sufficient height to put him out of danger. From this post he kept calling to his companions that the tiger was *hors de combat*, which caused them to rush forward again, amid such a Babel of tongues that it was useless attempting to give them any directions. Three times they did this, and three times the tiger endeavoured vainly to scale the heights, receiving on each occasion a spherical bullet from my gun. After the third shot, he retired into a thick bush, and there expired.

The elephants having now come up, I took Heera Guj, who, now that I was alone, was not troubled with the howdah, into the cover, and had the tiger placed on his back and sent home. We now decided to beat for the tigress, and when I told Roopa which bush she had broken from, and the line she had taken, he had no difficulty in making his plans. 'But,' he said, 'though some one is sure to see her, it is a great chance whether you will get a shot or not, for the jungle on ahead is of great extent, and nowhere so thick that tigers could have any favourite haunts in it. I will, however, take you to the best post, such as it is.' On this, he took me to a comparatively open plain, where the spur of a mountain ended in some large black stones, quite big enough to hide a few people sitting down. 'These stones,' said Roopa, 'lie exactly on the nearest path to the next really good jungle, and animals going from one fastness to the other generally pass by them.'

I did not think it likely anything would come of this drive, as this ground would have required a dozen guns to command it; still, it was a pleasant occupation to sit and watch the far distant beaters, who could be more or less made out perhaps as much as a mile off. Hurrichund was now in command, and as the cover was not thick or dangerous, he could do it very well. Mounted on the back of Ashmut Guj, his appearance was quite that of a great chief marshalling his forces.

It was very interesting to watch the driving of these hills, which rose like an amphitheatre around me. As each thick patch or up-running ravine was approached, Hurrichund would wave his turban, and the beaters would spread in the required direction, and beat it correctly. Once I could perceive a great commotion along a part of the line, and sounds of frantic shouting reached us as the tigress was viewed. Great efforts were now made to make her head towards me, but without success, and at last the chase had to be abandoned.

We now all assembled preparatory to returning to the bungalow, which was about three miles distant. I did not drive Ashmut Guj on this occasion, but sat at ease with Roopa and two other shikarries on the pad or broad mattress which constituted his saddle. Behind us walked Hurrichund at the head of fifty or sixty wild-looking beings, unclothed except as to their heads, which were decorated with long cloths twisted into loose turbans, containing stuff enough for a decent suit a-piece. To beguile the tedium of the route, Hurrichund began to relate all the circumstances of the beat. According to his own version, he was constantly at close quarters with the tigress. Whenever he reached a point of this kind in his narrative he mimicked the roaring of the royal beast. I thought as he did this that Ashmut Guj arched his back, and gave other signs of relishing the account. Warming with the recital, Hurrichund at last surpassed himself, and roared quite splendidly.

Like lightning, Ashmut swung himself round, elevated his ears, and prepared to charge.

Never shall I forget the scene that then ensued. The wild and breathless scampering—arms, legs, and turbans flying in all directions. Hurrichund's particular dread was an enraged elephant, so, casting his head-dress from him, perhaps as a bait for the monster, he fled as fast as his long, queer-looking legs could carry him. The ample fringe of dingy hair that hung all round his pale tonsured skull, rendered him fearfully conspicuous, and together with his great height would at once have made him the mark for the elephant had he pursued the flying throng. There were no rocks, trees, or other harbours of refuge within miles. In speed lay the only hope, and to make some one else last was the instinctive policy of each, as in this case the devil would certainly take the hindmost.

A race of a hundred yards, however, was sufficient to place Hurrichund, who was leading, far enough in advance of the main body of the fugitives to enable him to risk a glance over his shoulder. There stood Ashmut Guj immovable, so Hurrichund at once halted, and was immediately surrounded by all his followers.

For a few seconds the elephant and beaters stood confronting one another, and then the former, yielding to the repeated blows of his driver, and being unable to make out who it was that had insulted him, turned round, and resumed his way home.

It now occurred to me, as a distraction, to see what this beast would do if I, seated on his back, were to imitate a tiger charging. I was getting on very well, as I thought, when the mahout said, 'Every time you make that noise the elephant points his trunk over his back, and takes a long sniff, to inform himself as to which of his passengers is trying to vex him.'

I at once desisted from my thoughtless jokes, for although I did not care much for Ashmut Guj, still, as I intended to ride him in the absence of a better mount, it was clearly a mistake to set him against me. I was therefore quite quiet for the rest of the journey, and on arriving at the bungalow an hour afterwards I had quite forgotten the little incident. But not so Ashmut Guj. At the word of command he bent his hind legs, and allowed the three natives to slip off his back in succession. I was the last to dismount, and as I touched the ground the elephant rose with a swift movement, and aimed a fearful kick at me with his enormous club-like hind foot. I started forward, so as just to escape the blow, which would, of course, have annihilated me. Nor would this elephant ever forgive me for the indignity I had put upon him. Always at dismounting, he would try to rise, so as to repeat the manœuvre, and it was consequently necessary to make him kneel completely down before I got off. Nor would I ever feed him again from the hand, as I believe if he could have got hold of me he would have trampled me.

Of course, had it been a really good elephant, like Roghanath Guj, I should never have played any tricks upon him, or having done so, I would have persevered with endless pains till I had made it up. But I never intended to make use of Ashmut Guj again, so I thought the best way was to remain for the future on 'stand off' terms with him.

It was now time to look after the tiger I had shot in the morning. It had been deposited in a large empty outhouse, where no sun could penetrate. To this place I now repaired, and the skinning of the animal was at once proceeded with. From what I had observed previous to loading the tiger up on the elephant, I had thought that my first Express bullet must have penetrated the heart; but if so, how could the tiger have lived so long, and attempted so much afterwards?

As soon as the hide was removed, we dragged the body outside, and opened it. My chief skinner, Chowpatty, was not long in taking out the heart, and exposing it to view. It was completely shattered half-way through from top to bottom. This must have been done by the first bullet, or some might say the second, which was fired immediately after the first. The other three shots were far back, and were by round bullets from a twelve-bore gun. Now the contrast between the holes made by such different missiles is so great that the most inexperienced could not mistake one for the other. I can therefore only consider this a striking instance of the tenacity with which tigers sometimes cling to life, and as showing with what caution they should be approached when supposed to have received their death-blow.

It was now as late as the 19th of June, and the monsoon, or rains, should have been in full force by this time. This would have rendered the jungle uninhabitable, and all except metalled roads quite impassable. As yet, however, there had been no signs of the annual deluge, which is generally heralded by at least a fortnight of high winds, charged with damp and continually increasing volumes of black clouds scudding low over the surface of the parched earth and withered vegetation. This year all was fair and bright up to this late period, and as I had quite four days of leave left, I still hoped I might kill another tiger or two. So by Roopa's advice I tried the next day for the tigress belonging to the male animal which I had just despatched.

I was taken to what was considered the best spot for getting a shot, and here I was glad to find that rarity in these jungles, an excellent tree on which I could make a first-rate, all-round stand, and so high that I could at all events get my first shot in safety. I sat alone in the tree, and the beat was very well conducted by Roopa. All the round hills were beaten by different lines of skirmishers coming towards me. Some of these, more advanced than the rest, had got close up to me, and the others were not far off. From the unbroken calmness with which they had all advanced, I knew that the tigress had not been sighted, and could only suppose that we had not hit off her whereabouts on this occasion.

Just as I had come to this conclusion, I heard a tremendous roaring, and on looking in the direction the sound came from, there was the tigress going at a racing pace all along the line of beaters. I was the only person who was in a safe position, so I felt it would be unjustifiable on my part to take a snap shot at such a moment, as by so doing I should have exposed all these defenceless people to great danger. I therefore withheld my fire for a more favourable opportunity.

'What,' I said to Roopa, 'could have made the beast suddenly appear going at that mad pace?'

'Oh,' he said, 'it was most unfortunate; she was evidently creeping slowly in front of the drive, and was going to give you a nice chance, but a sounder of pig charged right down on her just at the last moment, and that was what set her off.'

We had many more beats through the day, but did not see her again, and we had to return disappointed to the bungalow.

And now suddenly the wind rose, and great black clouds began to fly across the heavens. It was to be feared the monsoon was coming, as it sometimes does, with a rush, as though to make up for lost time. Had I been sitting gasping in a dull military cantonment, I should have enjoyed the delicious change of atmosphere. So great was the difference, that it was as though one had travelled a thousand miles in half an hour. This great change took place at night, and for a time the darkness was such as could almost be felt. Then with a blinding flash of lightning, and a simultaneous crash of thunder, the rain descended in torrents that sounded like the rush of a river.

I looked out upon the landscape when it was brilliantly illuminated by the lightning. In a few moments what a surprising revolution had taken place! The drought-stricken plain of this very afternoon was now a sheet of water, for all the world like a lake. Nothing living was revealed to my gaze by the constant flashes of nature's electric light, except the huge black forms of the two elephants, who stood in the midst of the watery waste, looking the very picture of desolation. I say they looked wretched, for there was no reason why they should be so. To them nothing is more delightful after a hot day's work than to wallow all night in considerably deeper water than that in which they now found themselves. And I am certain that but for the vividness of the lightning, and the continued rattling of the thunder close overhead, they would have considered this one of the pleasantest nights of their lives. But no animals like to be in the open during a thunderstorm; all instinctively seek the shelter of trees or rocks, notwithstanding that the former are said to be such dangerous neighbours under the circumstances. The raging of the elements, however, seemed in no way to disturb the equanimity of Ashmut Guj; but Heera, as the illuminations waxed in brilliancy and the thunder in volume, could be seen during the prolonged flashes waving his trunk, and uneasily rolling his great body from side to side, till finally and unexpectedly I was greeted with a sort of dissolving view of this elephant disappearing into the jungle.

This was another instance of the desperate carelessness of mahouts. They must have well known that this animal feared thunder, and should at the first clap have laced up his hind legs with a long rope, instead of leaving him to his ordinary loose fastenings. The reader may think that I should have seen to this. But these elephants were Government property, and the two men in charge of each were supposed to know the habits, requirements, etc., of their own animals. And, indeed, the character of each elephant is so peculiarly its own, that it would be quite impossible for a comparative stranger to manage one successfully from the first, and in every situation. All that can be expected of one is to be always ready to render the mahout whatever assistance he may apply for from time to time. During the darkness of the night it would have been useless to try and recover the truant, and had the storm continued, as it might be expected to do at this time of the year, for several days, it would have been no easy task to get the beast back. Fortunately, however, the tempest, after lasting in full fury for about three hours, suddenly subsided.

The dawn broke, if not smiling, at any rate with comparative calm, and revealed Heera Guj standing also calm under the shelter of a neighbouring banyan tree of great size, off the lower branches of which he had supped all night, and was now breakfasting with undiminished appetite. He was at once taken possession of by his keepers, who sincerely believed that they themselves had been throughout the affair striking instances of prudence, promptitude, and courage, and certainly deserving, as the head man murmured, of 'bakhsheesh' (*i.e.* reward). Such is the native mind! Being thoroughly used to the people, I neither smiled nor spoke. The elephant was present, and all right; that was all I cared for. I now sent for Roopa, who was one of those exceptional characters that would have been a credit to any country. 'Well,' I said, 'Roopa, what do you think of the present state of affairs?'

'Well,' he said, 'you must, of course, pack up and hurry back to Neemuch, and be glad of every step you can make before more rain comes.'

I knew this was good advice, but as the sun now appeared among the many-coloured heavy clouds that were hastening like vast armies from the south-west, I felt there might be still a chance of falling in with the tiger of all others that I should have liked to have killed.

'Sir,' said Roopa, 'you must give it up, for after rain like this not a beater will go into the jungle for days to come, no matter what you may pay him; and even if the rain should hold up, after such a fall the bushes will have burst into leaf in that time, and then you know yourself nothing could be done.'

'But,' I said, 'why cannot you persuade these men to go and do one more beat to-day?'

'Sahib,' he replied, 'to do so now after this rain would be contrary to their dustoor' (*i.e.* custom).

At this word dustoor, a sort of faintness overcame me. Only those who have lived in the Far East may know the talismanic power of this odious and mildly tyrannical term. Mountains may be moved or oceans drained by engineering skill, but dustoor will hold its dominion as long as there are Indians to submit to its mysterious sway.

Since, then, retreat was decided upon, I endeavoured, by not losing a moment, to make it, if possible, a successful one. Now it depends altogether on circumstances whether forty-five miles—the distance from Gungarar to Neemuch—should be considered a long or a short journey. In this case all depended on the rain—whether we were to have any more, and if not, what might have been the effect of last night's deluge on the unmetalled track. One thing was very certain, namely, that if the downpour should come on again, I should have to travel to Neemuch on the back of an elephant, and leave the servants, kit, and camels for an indefinite time at the nearest villages. Camels are simply unable to move over the deep and slippery mud, which in the rains constitute almost the entire footing from one station to another throughout the greater part of India. When on really swampy ground, the front legs of these poor creatures slip outwards, till, I believe, the animal is sometimes split up. At all events, one might expect them to be fatally injured before they had gone a mile. Besides this, there were the numerous unbridged mountain torrents that crossed the road dozens of times, to be considered. It may be asked how other people travelled along this road at this season of the year. Well, the road was considered closed during the monsoon, and no one attempted to journey by it till the dry weather had come round again.

Having seen everything properly loaded up, and every animal and man belonging to me collected in one group, I mounted my horse, and led the way to the next Government bungalow, which stood midway between Gungarar and Neemuch. The road turned out better than I could have hoped. It had, of course, been marked out so as to avoid the lowest levels, and eight months of continuous baking had rendered the soil sufficiently thirsty to cause the absorption of most of the water that had fallen on it. Still, we had to be very careful, and our progress was so slow that the shades of evening were falling as we arrived at our temporary yet welcome little home.

Whilst waiting for dinner, I walked towards the place where all my animals were located, to see how they were getting on. As I approached Ashmut Guj, his mahout came to meet me, carrying with both hands a brown-looking object about the size of a small coal-scuttle. 'Behold, sir,' he said, 'the back tooth of the unhappy Ashmut; this is the second that I have seen fall out; who is now to chew the food of this ill-fated one?'

'Why,' I said, 'you must, of course.' And this was the only comfort I could give him. But in any case he did not have to perform this extra labour for long, as the elephant died a month or two after this catastrophe.

The rain fortunately still kept off, so the next morning at dawn we all took a hasty meal, and wended our slow and tedious way into Neemuch, where we arrived just in time for me to dress and dine with a number of kind friends whom I was very glad to see again. Thus ended my shooting trip of the year 1876.

Having got into a comfortable, spacious house, I naturally cried, 'Now let the rain come down.' But instead of doing so, the weather cleared up and became alarmingly fine. We seemed to be threatened with that truly awful calamity, a failure of the monsoon, which means famine on a scale that can happily never be approached in Europe. Not till the 7th of July was the anxiety of all classes turned into rejoicing. On that day the floodgates of heaven were opened, and the monsoon, though nearly a month behind its time, commenced in true orthodox fashion, thus ensuring plenty and prosperity for the coming year. I think every one enjoys the rainy season, in spite of the fever and other complaints which such a deluge naturally brings with it. The quantity of rain that falls over the great area watered by the south-west monsoon, varies greatly in different localities. In some mountainous regions, I am told, between two and three hundred inches may be obtained, whilst in other parts not more than twelve or fifteen will be registered. At Neemuch, about forty inches would be considered a good allowance. This may not sound very much for the annual rainfall, but as it all comes in about three and a half months, it can be understood that there is enough rain during that short period to entirely revolutionize the life of the previous eight months of drought, when the fiery sun seems to be ever shining in skies of brass.

Now all out-door pursuits, whether of business or pleasure, are made to depend on the state of the clouds. Throughout India this is the season of the 'Gym-Khana,' a weekly meeting of all the convivial and sporting spirits of the station. Horse-racing, polo, cricket, and various other games are indulged in on a piece of ground well laid out and kept up for the purpose. An open building, large enough to accommodate all the members and visitors, is erected in a suitable position, for purposes of refreshment or shelter whenever the rain comes on. Of course the weather is sometimes so bad that these *réunions* cannot be held, and then people have to fall back on purely indoor entertainments. At large stations where there are a good many ladies, balls and dances form a never-failing source of amusement. At Neemuch the fair sex were well represented, and consequently afternoon dances were much the fashion. Some of the houses were built with a sort of raised platform of white concrete resembling marble thrown out in front of the drawing-room windows, which opened on to it like the flooring of a large hall, only with nothing built over it. Here the ladies would float gracefully in their Watteau-like costumes, as the light waned, to the pleasant sounds of a military band playing the 'Lancers' or a 'quadrille.' On bright moonlight evenings such entertainments are often kept up till long after dark, and even then are only brought to a close by the rising of the chaperons *en masse*, who have for the last hour been mutely interrogating the heavenly bodies as to what the cooks can possibly be doing with the dinners at their respective homes.

Life was passing thus pleasantly with me during this monsoon, when orders were received that the native regiment with which I was doing duty was to march, as soon as the deluge should be over, to Delhi, there to take part in the magnificent pageant which was to be held at that place for the purpose of proclaiming Queen Victoria Empress of India, with the Asiatic title of Kaisar-i-Hind. What befell me on this and many other journeys, will be the subject of another volume.

END OF VOLUME I.